Karl-Heinz Hermsch

Feelings of anger

(How feelings arose and move people)

(Revised Edition)

© Karl-Heinz Hermsch 2023

Version: February 2026

Preliminary remark

There are, among others,

4 types, something consider.

(E.g. the content of a Non-fiction):

1. One cannot understand that.

2. You don't want to understand that because it doesn't fit your own worldview. *(So, not to the aims that created this.)*

3. You use your cognitive abilities to understand it.

4. One has judged beforehand and thinks one understands everything.

Suggestion

One way to extinguish fire and anger is to control your breathing.

In the form:

- *Breathe in for 4 moments*

- *Hold your breath for 2 moments, while saying: 'Expand your cosmos'*

- *Breathe out for 6 moments, slowly slipping into 'deep relaxation'.*

(More details in the last chapter: 'Satisfaction and meditation'.)

Prologue

To get some clarity, you could first ask yourself:

Why do I have this feeling of anger?

Have I not achieved an aim?

<table><tr><td>

Principle:

If you want to know your-self, ask about your aims.

</td></tr></table>

((For more details, see Chapter 6.)

Then: the first step - not giving in to your anger immediately - would be to ask yourself about the general attitude towards your feelings: **Could it be that you <u>always</u> trust them; considers them perhaps infallible?**

A help for the answer is one's own past: how often did feelings bring you to a conclusion, sometimes with a lot of persuasion - then it often turned out to be incorrect.

These experiences could lead to the healthy attitude of not always trusting feelings unconditionally.

The second step would be:

As with all problems in life, you should take a close look at the feeling.

This should make this clearer, and one could see that the absolute certainty it exudes only "counts" as an argument to convince man of the "truth of the feeling."

Feelings of anger can arise when aims are not achieved - because something was not or did not happen as expected or requested.

Therefore, this is a starting point for changing or avoiding feelings.

That is, to determine the decisive aims and then try to modify them.

Just looking closely at your emotions can make a difference! (Among other things, because one does not immediately carry out the blind reactions evoked by the feeling.)

Recommendation:

A general means of initially limiting negative outbursts of emotion is also the sentence:

"What happened had to happen as it happened."

((For more details, see Chapter 2.)

If you have recognized that the mood in yourself is based on an unachieved aim, then two points could help:

The first: Since what happened is in the past (which one cannot change), to say to oneself: "What happened had to happen as it happened."

The second point: To consider: What can I do about the trigger to better cope with this aim that triggered the negative feelings in myself?

For example, trying to change the aim in me, my expectations - because it is probably simply not possible

> or unrealistic to achieve
> it.

Everyone has feelings and intellectual systems that shape them - and can also lead astray through wrong aims.

While the mind is more easily altered using its cognitive abilities, feelings are more autonomous. They do not need to justify themself or be persuaded by knowledge.

Feelings form out of experience.

This strong role has been preserved in people to this day.

However, since every situation is more or less different from others, this can of course result in incorrect attitudes and decisions.

While one can think through situations cognitively, feelings often act immediately and de-

mand responses (via the Mid-point-Mechanics.)

((For more details, see Chapter 7.)

The feeling fools you - with more or less pressure - that you absolutely need something or should do something (because it is an aim that wants to be achieved).

Again, if you see a danger of drifting into the negative through feelings, **take a close look, especially those that are very pressing!**

And possibly try to change this for the future.

This is achieved less by persuasion with cognition, but by:

Feelings should be met with feelings!

So, create an emotional counterweight (aim) that builds up a special neural network that gradually creates new reaction

structures and finally takes over the function of the old midpoint.

In the form of imagining everything positive that you can achieve by not giving in to your feelings – and contemplating everything negative, especially in pictures, such as your own helplessness and possible later regret. regarding yielding. (The psyche likes to respond to pictures).

The old behaviour then continues to exist (because it is not completely erased), but usually loses more and more power and 'leadership'.

Contents

Starting point

Everyone has two sides: feeling and reason.

The feeling developed about 3.5 billion years ago from the first moment in which life arose and wanted to survive.

All further beings then arose with specific feelings (formed for survival). Insofar as they produced offspring, the feelings were also inherited.

The **mind** evolved much later (as head brain) through competition with other living beings for resources to survive.

Understanding means understanding a structure and its changes and drawing conclusions for yourself.

This is - in relation to the feeling - a much more complicated and extensive area that took a long lead time to develop.

Emotion (like the gut brain) affects more or less all areas of life and plays an essential role.

However, it can neither think nor reflect; it is not intelligent. It only acts on the basis of similarities in the past: feelings are therefore memories in order to react in a consistent way in apparently identical situations. What used to be positive or negative in the similar situations is transferred to today and a similar reaction is sought. As a result, feelings can exert a strong pressure that resists attempts at cognitive change.

So feeling and reason are often opposed to each other as opposites.

Now, as a rule, neither one side nor the other is absolutely right.

It follows that it would be healthy to strive for a union of these opposites.

So similar to how it is expressed in the Yin and Yang symbol.

Like cognitive experiences, feelings arise in the brain and are stored in the respective neural networks.

They guide people. In addition to cognition, emotional perception is the other pillar that controls people - although it has a lot of power.

Feelings range from fine-tuning (to do something precisely) to over-powering urges (when the brain judges it to be of the utmost importance) and are often stronger than reason; it's hard to resist them - as everyone knows. They can blind you completely.

The midpoints (neuron networks) create a world that is coordinated with an aim. This generates corresponding feelings that more or less urge to satisfy the aim.

If you have wrong aims in yourself, wrong, often unhealthy feelings are also generated.

(For more details, see Chapter 15).

Feelings can control people very well. Therefore, everything he does, experiences etc. is accompanied by it.

It is much more economical (as I said) to summarize important situations in feelings, which should later help in similar states to evaluate them more quickly than when the brain stores everything in front of a person in all details and from this picture would act.

Many variable feelings can overlap and form a pattern that has the character of a request in similar situations.

Regarding false aims: feelings are sometimes not properly attuned to the world. if e.g. for example, if your gut feeling says you should decide this or that one way or the other, then you cannot seldom later register that you made the wrong decision.

But the feelings are often right. So it's not that easy to spot false feelings. But if something very important is at stake, then it would be good to keep what has been said here clearly in mind and turn on the thinking. This activates the consciousness (the enhanced senses) at the same time, so that what the feelings want can be looked at more closely. And so, the brain – more precisely the midpoints – receives information from its feelings **and** thinking and thus the possibility to revise its decision.

Again, and again you experience feelings that tell you 100% that this or that is absolutely right and in order and that want to lead you there – sometimes with strong urges. However, if you are not an expert in the field (but also sometimes if you are an expert), you should possibly question these feelings critically (see above). Because the less you know about something, the more your feelings can fool you creatively.

The brain makes its own, sometimes erroneous, interpretations, thereby misleading people.

Depending on the value of the aim, feelings can be very strong. Especially when an essential value has to be given up. For example, when you're grieving. Here an old aim has to give way to a new one, namely the realization that something you loved is no longer there. The old aim creates the tears, the pain because it can no longer be reached.

So, when you're sad, going through the range of emotions, it's because of an aim that can no longer be reached. This works until you come to terms with it.

A quick comparison of the <u>principles</u> on which living beings, or artificial intelligence (AI), make statements:

(As I said, life began about 3.5 billion years ago from matter - together with the emergence of feelings that it controls.)

◆ Living beings (including humans) still prefer to use them to make judgments today.

◆ Artificial intelligence forms answers from facts - uninfluenced by feelings.

Feelings of anger

> Feelings arise through evaluating and carrying out aims.
>
> Countless numbers develop in order to enable people in the world to survive and to be able to adapt.
>
> If you are clear about this, you can try to intervene in the process if you do not want something:

• Look at the 'wrong' aim; what exactly does it want to achieve? For what reasons did it arise?

• Form a counter-aim out of feelings, which is interlinked with this - that is, always activated at the same time - and thus devaluates the wrong.

> The human being is so knitted that he often gives in to his feelings when they

press him. The reason lies in the early days of the most primitive living beings billions of years ago, from which humans ultimately developed. There were no cognitive abilities here, only the feelings that developed from the information of the existing senses and guided the living beings. Therefore, feelings can also have this urgent character, because they especially want to ensure survival.

As a result, trust has burned into people's feelings and they may have difficulties deciding against them.

In the course of evolution (thousands of years later), cognitive skills then developed. With these one could recognize laws and then apply them in a targeted manner.

While feelings generally go according to the motto: What is similar can also be used for similar problems and solutions, cognition, for example, looks at these similarities, differentiates and seeks to see the rules according to which they run in order to change them, or replace other processes.

Summarized:

Living beings, and of course humans too, decide primarily on the basis of their feelings.

The reason for this lies in the original structures, because; at the very beginning of life there was still no cognitive decision, only sensory information recordings, which later, depending on the organism, showed up as feelings.

So, in the course of evolution, feelings kept the predominance in terms of decisions based on the respective aims.

In mammals, and especially in humans, the frontal lobe (lobus frontalis), which is responsible for cognition, arose and developed more and more - because he was successful with it. Over time, it grew in volume. In humans, it now makes up more than 30% of the cerebral cortex.

But since the brain is permeated by stored feelings, these have a very great influence and often weaken or suppress - via the central point mechanics - the conclusions of the mind.

This can be seen very well in the feeling (the belief) in one's free will or that the person makes the decisions with his consciousness (and not the brain).

Neither is and cannot be scientifically proven.

There is no question that feelings have a central, healthy function for humans.

But: There is no question that they do not always make the right decisions.

And: Restricted emotional life (often genetic) can have significant disadvantages for people, similar to the consequences of frontal lobe damage.

When anger rises in you, it can help (as I said) to be aware of two facts - of course only if the anger has not completely blinded you:

▶ You are the way you are.

▶ What happened had to happen as it happened.

(That doesn't mean that you should become phlegmatic, nor that you shouldn't work on yourself or your environment for the future.)

It doesn't do much to be angry with yourself, for example. This certainly does not change the past and may only allow your blind revenge (including yourself) to run free. You decrease your self esteem and self-confidence.

As a rule, in life it is like this: If something does not work out, then you should think about how you can do it better in the future.

And that should also apply to his anger.

Since we now know (which is to be hoped) that people are controlled by themselves - their psychological aims - it makes sense to ask about those who triggered the anger (or anger).

Now that it is well known (and hopefully so) that people are driven by themselves—their psychological aims — it makes sense to ask about those who caused the anger.

Once you have discovered the aims, you have an advantage: they can possibly be influenced so that they can no longer throw you off track with these emotions.

I think it's better to look at your anger first than to blindly submit to it.

And – in order to avoid similar behavior in the future, one should develop a strategy for self-knowledge.

Once again: Anger means that an intended aim has not been achieved and from the inside of the person the request, the urge to achieve this (or an alternative) can still arise - no matter how or by what means.

The anger is often projected outward; to other people, other living beings, inanimate objects that are supposed to be to blame. Often also on the fate that it is after you or on evil forces.

It influences the mood and creates sadness or resignation up to depression.

Unfortunately, one often does not get the idea that the anger is triggered by one's own aims or attitudes.

Because, as I said: many of the reactions occur because of wrong aims in oneself. With regard to

one's own expectations of people and the environment.

Quite a few people get angry and curse each other if it does not lead to the result that one was striving for.

If one conquers this anger, and moves calmly further in the direction of the healthy aim, finally achieves it (e.g. through compromises), then one is satisfied in the psyche and proud of oneself.

Everyone has ideals of themselves - how they want or should be. This includes also often not to make mistakes, to be perfect.

With regard to these causes, you could find what you are looking for with your reference persons, the people you grew up with, the culture in which you lived or now live, and with the people you are with now (because the idealized aims often cause anger if they are not achieved).

For example, if you are angry that something did not work as you expected, then an unconscious metaphysical or mystical belief, which has smuggled itself in the course of genetic development, often plays a role. Here you could make it clear: Objects have no will and don't want to annoy you.

> There are ways to avoid anger (as I mentioned):
>
> ▶ Saying to yourself (as explained above): "What happened had to happen as it happened", because everything happens on the basis of substances that run according to laws.
>
> ▶ And / or try to research the trigger, to reconsider, to ask what part you have in it and how you can change, possibly to modify the aim or to give up completely.

In order to get to know each other better, you could observe yourself (with your SELF, which is also located in the brain). One would, inter alia, find that the same processes often occur. Here would also be an approach to changing one's habits.

Because you are of course dependent on your psyche. And for harmony and balance, it's good to get along with yourself. Mental contentment and balance is shown when the midpoints harmonize with each other.

This is not achieved by violence, nor by punishing oneself with curses.

Once again: Since the reactions (anger and anger) ultimately come from one's own point of view and attitude, one should usually start with oneself when making changes. A solution could be created by asking how I could behave more moderately and appropriately in similar situations.

Once you have found an answer, you could link it to the spontaneous reaction.

More precisely: Form an aim with this answer, so that every time the impulse wants to evoke the negative behaviour, this is also activated and thus dampens and regulates one's own behaviour.

If one succeeds in doing this, then the anger will also decrease in the future because the aims have been defused.

Since we are all driven by aims, of course, creating new aims is far more effective than curse yourself.

This is the key to change.

A little suggestion for dealing with unpleasant incidents that had happened:

If you go by the motto: What happened had to happen the way it happened, then there really is no point in getting angry.

Questions like: "How could you do that?" "Can't you pay attention?" and similar allegations would no longer be asked regarding the past.

The further and more intensively one investigates the situation in which something happened, the clearer it becomes that it had to happen exactly as it did.

In the future, of course, people will behave differently in similar situations once they have learned and gained experience - only in the situation at that time there was only one possibility (due to legal processes).

There are many, if – then. Only for the past, i.e. if something happened, they are of no use.

But of course you can use them for the future.

So: why do you get angry?

Because an aim was not achieved.

Why not?

Because it was not possible with respect to the environment or the people or the inadequacy with regard to oneself.

Is this anger useful or harmful?

Usually the latter.

How could something be changed in relation to this aim in the future?

Mostly, to modify the desired aim: So when you can overcome yourself to influence or change your own aim.

An advice:

> You are who you are, so accept yourself as you are – if you cannot change without harming yourself.
>
> **Because you are what you are - i.e. your brain is (what abilities and possibilities it has).**
>
> In addition, think of the motto: what happened had to happen the way it happened.
>
> So your brain had to become what it is now too. And be as it is according to your change request (i.e. same or changed).
>
> **And you can only change yourself through your brain (for example with your SELF, which, as I said, is also in the brain) - if this has the ability to do so.**

Another little analysis: When someone is angry about something they did themselves, it is often the case that at the moment when they are angry, the situation at the time comes back to them like a flash flooded. So, he acts as if he just did that.

Summary:

> **Anger is always triggered by aims that are in one and have formed neural networks - focal points.**
>
> **One solution, as I said, would be to make this aim clear and try to find out why and through what it was formed.**
>
> **Then one could consider how to reduce the anger or stop acting:**

- Is the aim really that important?

- Is it just an ideal or a wish?

- How could it be modified?

- Don't you accept yourself the way you are?

And finally, a word about brooding. (The word comes from digging: wanting to bring more and more to light by thinking about it, in order to find the causes, for example for a behavior.

"Definition (Wikipedia): Rumination is a form of thinking in which thoughts revolve around several topics or a specific problem without coming to a solution."

It usually saps energy and doesn't do anything unless you think about the incident, the topic, etc. to find out what the aims were and then change them.

To do this, you try to put yourself in the position of the time as accurately as possible. The better one succeeds in this, the more clearly one can see that this had to happen exactly as it did.

This has two advantages:

- The brooding stops.

- You learn to understand the world and yourself better; how the laws of that time had worked.

A suggestion:

What you should avoid as far as possible is to ask yourself with a reproach or self-accusation of guilt: "How could you do that!?

Because:

1. It had to happen because of the laws.

2. As a rule, it is often difficult to put yourself back precisely into the situation of the past with all the circumstances and feelings.

3. If you really managed to do that, you would usually come to the conclusion that it had to work exactly like this.

4. In order to achieve a change, it is sufficient to generate a different reaction for similar situations in the future - if necessary, to practice this in the 'dry state'.

And finally: If one does not come to a conclusion one way or another, then it is important to finally get rid of the brooding yourself (from this midpoint-circle). - For example through meditation or a similar behaviour that captivates attention.

Again: The way to the solution is to recognize your aims.

> "CP" represents countless conver-
> sations partner with whom I have
> discussed the topics for many
> years.

The ability to let go of the past

(What happened had to happen as it happened)

(Conversation about)

With the topic:

> Substances and Laws
> Blockages
> Conscience
> Fate
> Metaphysics

People are not machines.

The difference: living beings are primarily guided by <u>emotional</u> aims that lie within them. Here, survival and producing offspring play the central role.

The fact that everything had to come the way it came is documented from two sides:

- Identical parts under identical circumstances always result in identical structures. "

- With the statistical probability calculation, mathematicians can make very precise predictions about quantum systems. This would not be feasible if lawlessness prevailed here.

Serenity and tolerance follow involuntarily from the

Some people spend part of their lives cursing what's going on in the environment, or resenting themselves.

They are not satisfied - their aims have not been met - this affects their mood.

It would be healthy to say to yourself: "What happened had to happen as it happened."

How much more serenity would there be if you could implement this sentence and come to terms with it!

Because nobody can change the past.

The central point for inner flexibility is: Accept the world as it is - if you cannot change it.

It is liberating to be left by the shadows of the past.

(Anyone who succeeds in showing the precursors to the situation that led to this can prove this. With this method one can become absolutely clear that it had to happen exactly as it did.)

"It strikes me again and again how quickly you can break away from it when something hasn't turned out the way you expected - for example when anger rises in you," said CP. "That comes from your worldview?""

"I tell myself the motto: 'What happened, had to happen as it happened', and usually notice how the tension caused by the anger dissolves.

From my point of view, this is very healthy: I am not trapped by the midpoint of anger and can restructure relatively quickly. If it makes sense, I can focus on solutions to deal with what caused the trouble in similar situations in the future. If I continued to be caught in the midpoint of anger, it would block my restructuring. I would waste energy because I quarrelled with the past, with what had happened. Of course, I cannot change the past. "

"The key to achieving its aims is flexibility; not being hindered by wrong aims, such as anger about the past? "

"That way I can solve myself faster and use the gained capacities to reach my aims," I nodded.

"However: the more something moves me, the harder it becomes for me to neutralize it with the sentence: 'What happened, had to happen, how it happened'.

Like a mother whose son was murdered said, 'I know. that I cannot change the past - but the sadness stays with me'".

"Decisive for the right reaction is therefore always able to detach from the past?" CP hooked.

"That's the key point."

"But are not you sometimes mad at what happened, what happened to you? Does not that sound like it? Do you never complain about fate? "

"Why should I do that? Everything that happened had to happen the way it did.

Fate - or God or 'heaven' or whatever, blaming people for what happened to you - is neutral.

That is, nothing that happened to you has been caused by some higher power especially for you. Neither in the negative nor in the positive. "

"So, you are not, like some people, upset with fate that has given you the negative?"

"No. In addition, I have to say: The so-called 'Negative' is actually negative only by my respective attitude - not in itself, and not from every perspective. So, I get annoyed when my expectations are not met. The starting point for the solution is to withdraw or change my expectations. If I succeed, the anger will also be resolved. "

"So, the central point is the inner attitude?"

"Yes. That's why the sentence is so important: 'Know yourself', recognize your way of thinking and try to modify it when the aims are wrong."

"I have to ask again: Isn't it the case that, despite knowing that it had to happen the way it happened and the solution you have just outlined, you are sometimes angry or frustrated and find it difficult to overcome these feelings?"

"Of course, the feelings are not necessarily turned off by the knowledge, yes.

But that does not change the fact that everything had to happen the way it did. And of course, that in me then these feelings, such as anger occurs. "

--- substances and laws---

"You believe that there are only substances and laws that cause everything?"

"Yes, that's the way the world works: Everything consists of substances that run according to laws. Everything is a sequence of structures, constellations that are subject to certain laws that are also in them.

And therefore, everything had to happen as it happened, because the law of the respective value structure allowed only this and no other possibility.

It is my deepest conviction that this motto is irrefutable.

Therefore, you should take the world as it is - if you cannot change it - and not fight against it."

"Substances" do you define how? "

"'Substances' are elementary particles, structures, atoms, neutrinos, molecules, neurons, crystals, liquids, gases, cells, living things, brains, forces, facts, things, living things, ideas, ecosystems, stars, star systems, galaxies, etc.", he answered. "In addition, they are also considered as virtual substances in states of empty spaces (the vacuum in space)."

"So, everything?"

"Yes," I nodded, "invariably. Everything in the content of the universe is considered a substance: on a large scale, like galaxies - which are relatively tiny in relation to infinity - or on a small scale, like elementary particles. And of course, everything in humans.

"And 'laws'?

"'Law' means that identical parts - or waves - always give identical structures under identical circumstances.

Laws are properties of substances that, viewed in isolation, are unchangeable unless something is added to or removed from the substances.

And that means that everything can only proceed in a very specific lawful form."

"Substances and laws belong directly and inseparably together?" CP asked.

I nodded. "Yes, there are no substances without laws, you cannot separate or change them. The formula: substances = laws is universal.

> **1. Identical substances in identical circumstances always give identical results.**
>
> **2. The reason for this is that everything is governed by unchangeable laws.**

> **3. If you change substances or circumstances, then other laws also appear.**

Therefore, it is nonsensical to be mad at fate or anything higher, or to quarrel with it. "

Many people have difficulties with the past," I continued, "with what happened. They cannot detach themselves; they cannot let go; neither from your own past or from what happened in the world.

This is often a mistake, because - you should always be aware of this, also or just because it seems natural - the past cannot be changed!"

"Then you actually do not need to apologize if you did something wrong? Because what happened, had to happen that way! "

"Well, an important point in my ethics is respecting the world, the values of others. This includes especially the feelings. If they were hurt by my behavior, I should apologize for it - if only for the sake of harmony (also

50

within me). Likewise, if I have done damage; that I then try to make up for it.

I put my hands on the table.

In any case: With this motto it is easier to accept and let go of the past. And it can help to calm any anger."

--- blockades ---

"So: In order not to be mentally and physically hindered by the past; to remain able to act ", repeated GP," it is of particular advantage to be able to break away from it as quickly as possible, to be free to act; to act on what is currently necessary to achieve one's aims. "

"Right," I nodded, "to be free and to stay: this also includes, in particular, to detach themselves from the ideas, desires that prove to be unfulfillable."

"So, change expectations."

"Exactly because some of the old attitudes can be associated with feelings of disappointment, anger, sadness that hinder new, appropriate attitudes."

"These block the right behaviour to achieve its aims?"

"Naturally. The freedom of action is blocked. Because that's exactly what it's all about: being able to be flexible in order to be able to adapt."

"And the motto mentioned at the beginning is particularly suitable."

"Exactly. When you are angry with what happened in the past and complain about it loudly, then it is like shouting a stone: Because the cause of what had happened, were just substances, according to the laws expired.

So the point of anger should not be to quarrel with fate, to make reproaches, but to modify one's own attitude, one's behaviour. In a word: one's aims."

"But a lot of people don't see it that way."

"That's probably so. They want to take revenge, they cannot forgive others and themselves, they cannot forget insults, they cannot cope with defeats.

A mistake of the people is, as already said, that they often cannot take areas that are not to be changed as they are.

And in this futile struggle - to change oneself, the others and the world - they rub themselves up.

Often through unhealthy aims, which they have taken over during their development, for example, from caregivers and society.

How much energy is often spent and tied up to maintain the negative view of the past! "

"You mean, that if these people could see and accept the motto - and most of all - be able to solve themselves - then they could use those energies for themselves and others to shape the future better?"

"Naturally. But so, they remain in their midpoints, such as the self-reproaches: 'How could you do that'?

If they asked this question in the sense that they could avoid similar behaviour in the future that would be perfectly healthy.

But this question often becomes a rhetorical one that can be repeated endlessly and torments people. They are trapped by themselves for a long time: they cannot change the past and do not make the future any better for the reasons just mentioned. "

--- conscience ---

"This behaviour is also triggered, among other things, by their conscience?"

"Yes, through the values that they have in them, that shape them and tell them by their feelings what is right or wrong. This core of human beings is often so strong and offers considerable resistance to change that man lives in it as in a prison.

Similarly, if you feel you have to take revenge on other people for their actions: this revenge behaviour will always have an impact on yourself and a torture. And this vicious circle will continue as long as they cannot be solved."

"And could they change that if they saw that everything that happened had to happen the way it did?"

"That would be a way," I nodded.

"I think it's hard to go through life and look at it according to this motto. Because: Of course, you have your likes and dislikes. And you cannot just ignore that; the feelings come up and shape one. "

"Of course, you are quite right. I'm actually only concerned with a basic truth. That manifests itself in the 'motto'. "

"But it's actually a very good reason, you do not want to be vindictive," CP said.

"Sure," I nodded, "but there are many who want to be vindictive - for example, to enjoy the feelings of their own righteousness.

I mean: the one who cannot be attached to the negative past, but who can take her as it was, can be lucky. This is the way he can turn his attention to the present and the future -

largely negatively unencumbered. The past devours less energy.

Incidentally, even what I'm seeing is almost a thing of the past and had to be done as it happened. "

"You mean that, e.g., our conversation, which we are leading at this moment, is already past in the next moment? "

"Yes - and had to happen exactly as it happened."

"It's a strange thought to know that I had to say exactly what I just said."

"This view is certainly unfamiliar. But the very phrase you just said came from the aims of expressing your feelings in this way."

--- fate ---

"People who believe say, 'God determines fate', or 'People have their fate with God in their own hands'," CP changed the subject.

"That's the unrealistic thing about faith. You can try to make the most of everything and be happy if you succeed with it - but no matter if you have had success or failure, what happens then must be because of the substances and laws as it happens, and not because a god so wills.

So, people have their fate in their hands only to a limited extent; conditioned by the possibilities that they have.

Do you see the difference? On the one hand the belief in something supernatural, which can intervene at will in any event, without having to worry about any natural processes. For example, with a 'wave of the hand' to stop a tsunami heading for the coast, to stop an earthquake abruptly, or to bring a volcanic eruption to a sudden standstill. On the other hand, the realistic attitude that there is nothing supernatural that can intervene in natural processes.

It is the arrogance of people that we do not see, do not want to see that, like everything in the universe, we only proceed according to substances and laws.

Many 'seekers of knowledge', philosophers, religious founders, etc. said,

'My action was determined by a higher power'. These people are wrong! Action is never determined by a higher power, but is done on the basis of substances and laws. "

"Many people actually make a higher-level authority - say God - responsible for their fate," CP added.

"Again, it's just the neutral substances and laws that have led to something. But that can often, as I said, among other things not be seen by the vanity of people: that we are no more than anything else in the universe. "

"There are many people who say it's utter nonsense to say, 'what happened had to happen the way it happened'."

"Well - they simply lack the ability to analyse their behaviour."

--- metaphysics ---

"Why do so many people believe in God, mysticism, and similar supernatural?"

<blockquote>The concept of the head, the leader, whom one trusts, has an essential part in the primordial structures. This was</blockquote>

particularly important for living beings, such as prehistoric humans, in order to have aims, such as role models, in order to survive as best as possible.

This is where, with a high degree of probability, the actual cause from which the term "God" was formed can be found.

Since this is deeply anchored in the nature of people, it is shaped in the presence of the aims of subordinating oneself to someone, especially through feelings.

"And, the fact that there is something mystical, supernatural, God, was an absolute truth to the primitive human beings that gave them their feeling, otherwise they could not explain themselves to the world, which will eventually become established in the genome or epigenetics have, and emotionally continues in our primordial structures.

Then: After procreation, the new living entity may feel its surroundings as something diffusely overpowering in which it is bound, that gives it security, and has all the power. Also essential is the so-called 'magic phase' between the ages of 3 and 5 years. The feelings experienced here affect more or less later in life.

Depending on the plant and the culture in which it grows up, it will shape this feeling and make it more or less concrete. Here is always the experience of the feelings that it has made at the beginning of his life, have a strong value."

"That's how we create structures like 'God', right?"

"And all the creations of the brain in this way," I nodded, "which among other things have already caused so much horror in the world."

"Will this ever change?"

"I do not think so, most people are not ready to recognize themselves - much easier and 'nicer' is to stay in their wrong aims, feelings.

It is like this: What happened had to happen as it happened. "

Guilt, responsibility
and justice

(conversation about)

With the topic:

Forgive

> Here are two interesting perspectives
> on this topic.

- What happened had to happen as it happened.

- That the feelings of vengeance and retribution arise from the original structures of the human being.

"You said that everything is predetermined, because everything, including humans, consists of substances and laws, and everything is a successive

61

leap of structures. That is, everyone had to do exactly what he did. He ultimately had no choice! "

"That's right," I answered.

"But then nobody would ever blame."

"'Guilty' in the sense that he could have done something different, not."

"But a person can decide for himself whether he, for example, wants to take the right or left path! Doesn't he have that freedom? "

"Of course, the human can decide which way he wants to take," I nodded. " But basically, he has no freedom. Freedom is just an ancient human dream. For whichever direction he decides, he drops them according to the substances in them, more precisely: aims that are subject to very specific laws. These are in him from conception or have formed in the course of his life. These substances and laws bring about his decision."

"Is a society conceivable," CP asked, "who knows no guilt and, consequently, does not punish anyone for his wrongdoing?"

"Of course not," I replied. "No society can do without a legal system. And you have to make sure that the laws of society are respected. 'Guilt' means yes: the legal obligation to perform, to make amends. "

"But isn't it unjust to punish someone who has broken a law of society? Because according to your theory, everyone had to do what they did!"

"Right. But whether something is just, that is, right or wrong, can always be said in terms of an aim. And if that means maintaining the order of a society with certain laws, then it is fair to punish the lawbreaker. "

"What are 'right' and 'judging '?"

"Right comes from direction and is agreement thing between humans. Starting from the aim of 'knowledge', no one is to blame for what he did, because the natural substances and laws compelled him to do so. But if you start from the aim of keeping a society together, then the perpetrator must be to blame because he violated man-made laws that he should respect. This is to discourage him or others who want to do something similar from repeating such behavior. It is perfectly clear that nobody can change the past. Consequently, no one can be convicted. One can only condemn someone to make up for what he has done and can be punished so that he does not do it again. "

""Can't someone," CP said, "who was convicted, say anyway, 'It was unfair to punish me, because I had to do what I did, after all, everything is pre-determined! Isn't that an excellent excuse for his actions?"

"Sure, he can say that. But then you can also reply: 'There was no other way that we condemned you. We had to do what we did. Everything is pre-determined! '"

"What about the responsibility?" CP asked now.

"Responsibility means that people are accountable for their actions or omissions, i.e. they feel responsi-ble. He learns this through his so-

cialization process, which trains the conscience, together with the aims that lie within him from the original structures. Emotions in particular play a major role here."

"Could one develop a natural behavioural context that is valid for all humans? "CP wanted to know now.

"You mean a natural law that everyone is subject to? A right for all to derive from nature? "

"Yes."

"You can't do that. Because 'law' is defined by aims and these can be very different. "

"But aren't that what people are striving for?"

"They seek to establish their own behavior that they see as positive, and they want others to conform and have a similar set of values. The more related we are to others in terms of inner values, the more we like them, and vice versa. People like to see their own scale of values in such a way that nature or God created it as the right one."

"But doesn't this always lead to con-flicts between people, societies and cultures?"

"That's how it shows the history."

"Another question: If it should turn out that everything actually runs according to substances and laws, so that humans have no free will, then would not many legal systems have to be rewritten? Because these are still based on the fact that people can choose freely and have to atone for their guilt that they have incurred. "

"That should actually be so," I replied, "but it won't be, because the people who believe in free will, will probably always be far in the majority and dominate the jurisdiction. For example, the question of culpability: Under it, lawyers understand whether the perpetrator was at the time of the action in full possession of his mental powers to understand the injustice of his act. In other words, whether he could have prevented his actions with his free will.

But the substances and laws have led to this action, it had to be done as it happened! That is why I understand culpability to mean that the perpetrator should make amends for his crime as far as possible.

Well, it would be interesting to find out how the respective legislatures and judges came to assume that humans have free will," I continued, and then immediately gave the answer myself: "Traditionally and especially probably from the experience with themselves. Because they believe and think they feel that they make their own decisions of their own free will, although this may not have been examined by them at all! They simply assumed it, presumably because otherwise they would be deprived of an important legal basis."

"That sounds like arbitrariness," it came to CP's mind.

"Well - you could call it that because there is no evidence of free will."

It takes a lot of love for the truth and the ability to also see one's negative sides, i.e. to get closer to one's own psychology in order to come to the conclusion that one ultimately has no free will. Above all, this includes the ability to analyse oneself and one's own behaviour. But the biggest obstacle is: These people want to believe in their freedom! You are at the midpoint of this belief.

If you really want to understand, you have to put yourself in the exact moment of the crime: What was the perpetrator's structure like at the time and what was his environment like exactly.

The more precisely one can put oneself in the position of the situation at that time and feel it, the better one can understand it and inevitably comes to the conclusion, if one can understand it exactly, that it had to happen exactly as it did happen.

Of course, lawyers see it differently - because they are shaped by different aims (especially by the history of their respective jurisprudence).

They're neither scientists nor psychologists. They are fed by what they have learned; Among other things, to condemn the perpetrator because they assume that people have free will (without being able to prove it, of course), and could have done it differently at the time of the crime.

To understand this accordingly, would probably exceed the abilities of the judges.

If you want to imagine a situation identical to an earlier one, then that is probably simply impossible. Because:

> 1. It is too diverse

> 2. It is influenced by the current circumstances.

And so they judge according to previous practice, also because society demands it. "

--- forgive ---

"That reminds me, that it is said: 'To understand everything means to forgive everything.' That would fit well with your attitude."

"Yes, that's the way to put it - though, in everyday life, that's hardly possible for the reasons I mentioned earlier. In general, society has to punish infringements in order not to violate its structure. And that is exactly what the individual does to repair his damaged world and preserve stability. "

EMPATHY DON'T LEAD NECESSARILY TO SYMPATHY

Empathy is the ability to put yourself in someone's shoes. The sentence "What happened had to happen as it happened" also helps. In the past, people had to be what they were - and must be who they are in the present. The more empathy you have, the better you can understand the other person.

At the same time, the other will usually become more open when he feels so that one can understand him.

The respective aims are decisive. If one is empathic, then the aim is to understand the other person in their being, to put oneself in their shoes.

But whether you find the other person sympathetic is another matter.

To say "what happens must happen how it happens" does not mean that you approve of everything the other person did. It just says that what happened had to happen as it happened.

All human emotions and feelings in one are still there. Only they are more or less relativized by the knowledge that everything had to happen as it happened.

Of course, I would never approve of murder or similar crimes. But I know that everything had to happen as it happened. Accordingly, my reactions and judgments are more tolerant.

The sentence: "What happened 'had to happen as it happened" should not be an excuse, but a sober, irrefutable explanation regarding the situation at the time.

Tolerance means that you have to endure or have to endure what happened, also because you cannot change the past. Tolerance also means that you shouldn't take revenge blindly. And that you should possibly be considerate. Respect in the literal sense; that you look back on the past.

The ideal would be to punish the perpetrator only to the extent that he or someone else does not do this again. But since we are all human, with our feelings and emotions, our values and attitudes, this ideal will often not be achieved.

And one more word: It is not that you are not free in your actions and decisions. - However: Of course, one cannot be free in the true sense, because: what happened had to happen as it happened.
On the other hand, you are free to make decisions about the present and the future because you don't know what needs to happen.

THAT SOME FIND DE-ESCALATION SO DIFFICULT

Because you are too focused on yourself. Because you don't try to empathize with the other person. Because you want to be right. Because you really want to achieve your aims.

Conflicts arise due to different aims between people.

Certain patterns have formed for conflict resolution that one has learned or adopted (e.g. from role models).

The most unfortunate solution is violence. Because violence usually breeds violence, and this in turn breeds violence. This creates a spiral that creates a lot of suffering for everyone involved.

Patterns have been learned and can also be unlearned again. One way of doing this is by trying to recall situations that created or reinforced these patterns.

Why do many people use violence?

• Because they had violent people as role models.

• Because they think they are strong and it's the easiest way.

• Because they learned it in the family.

• Because they grew up in a social environment for which violence as a way of resolving conflicts was normal.

Resolving conflicts should always start with acknowledging the other person, taking them for what they are.

The ideal solution would be to seek a solution to the conflict together with the other.

Among other things, it would be helpful for a de-escalation to keep in mind:

• "What happened had to happen as it happened" (this way you don't judge, avoid assigning blame),

• Finding the right words, using descriptive phrases – primarily naming the other person's feelings – that start with an 'it' and contain no accusation. For example: "It seems..." or: "It looks like..." and then pausing to give the other person the opportunity to respond (this is how you focus on the situation and don't attack the other person)., and gets information from and about him),

• try to see the situation from the other person's perspective (this puts your own point of view into perspective and you can understand the other person better),

• Remain friendly and speak calmly (this shows the other person that you don't see aggression as a solution).

Appendix:

Dictators

A dictator is characterized by the fact that he ignores the aims of others insofar as they do not serve his interests.

He follows any opposition and does everything in his power to eliminate it. His means are violence and lies.

You won't find de-escalation in him - unless it serves his own purposes.

I.e. he is trapped in his world. And often feels like the chosen one.

Manipulating and exploiting are among his knitting patterns.

There are dictators not only in politics, but in all areas of life. However, these cause the greatest damage for many people there.

Aims

With the topics:

> Gestalt psychology
>
> Universal scholar
>
> Awareness Restriction
>
> Thinking habits
>
> Life attitudes
>
> Fear of death
>
> Thirst for knowledge

Aims (synonymous often values) consist of networks of synapses and neurons. These act as knitting patterns and mark or generate a path when activated. For this they structure the people and the world.

"You say all living beings are aim-oriented. How did you come up with that?" *CP* was curious.

"I wondered why people do what they do. And I have observed again and again that aims (as midpoints) shape people – as long as they are in the waking state of attention."

"And outside of wakefulness?"

"Are you in sleep, or similar states in which the midpoints have slackened and the brain structure changes drastically.

The difference between to be awake and sleep is that in the former the midpoints provide structure; The frontal lobe has a significant share in the aims sought here. Whereas they are partially reduced to zero during sleep (the forehead brain is then partially blocked - such as the logical functions). So, the midpoints have little influence on the brain, which can therefore conjure up the strangest images. Not infrequently it is somehow stimulated emotions that are experienced unbridled as reality with vivid fantasies.

Other mechanisms and laws are active.

But of course, everything continues according to substances and laws - only according to other aims."

"How do you define aims?"

"Form a structure that leads to the desired endpoint of a path. For this, two things are needed: First, man must form a structure in himself and he must see the world in a structure that shows a suitable path. And so, do all living beings because their original aim is survival. "

"That is, the living entity structures itself, brings in a different shape?" Asked *CP*.

"No, the respective aim is this form".

If you want to recognize your-self, ask about your aims.

The most important point is their nature: if they are not fulfilled, depending on the momentary or general value in a feeling self, they still urge to be reached somehow - even with alternatives.

"Aims are very important in your theory building," said C*P*.

"In fact, everything is structured by it," I nodded. "Take the system life. In every living being, there is a spectrum of aims that relativize, detach, connect with each other, form co-operative groups, cover up, wrestle for supremacy, and organize themselves into a partially alternate hierarchy. Aims are added, others change or go out. Each target has, or generates, its opponent, if other targets are touched and run the risk of being compromised. And every action takes place through a set of aims that each develop structures, compromise, reinforce or weaken. Many aims change in the course of life, except for the very low-lying, for example, the life instinct. This one always remains, even if you are very old."

"That sounds very complicated," said CP.

"It is," I nodded again. "The whole system is incredibly diverse and nested. That makes it so difficult to tell exactly where the driving forces of action come from.

Every behavior, if traced back, will have its origin in the urge to live. In most cases, there are many intermediate steps between this and the current behaviour. That's why it's often hard to find the connections. But the younger a living being is, the easier it is to detect them. In the course of his life man differentiates more and more. It expands more and more, depending on what aims it carries within itself."

"Can you never get to the bottom of the psyche?"

"Not in the smallest detail. But if you want to try to recognize yourself, it helps to know that everything is shaped in one of aims – like those of the SELF, which are also in the brain and play an essential role.

Ultimately, people are always circling around the same aims, only the content is different. The ultimate aim is, as a rule, the life instinct, which, it seems, always wants to grow, wants more and higher, closely followed by the aim of orientation, showing man his environment, which is of value to him, in positive or negative Meaning, in order to be able to react accordingly. The most important design factor is then the group - starting with two people - the society in which one lives. The aim of being recognized is arguably one of the strongest in life. Thus, the society in which one lives can totally become one's own world, that is, it can express one's aims, in other words: Values that have been anchored in the socialization process can absolutely shape you and cannot lead to other aims in this regard."

"You say there's no life without a midpoint?"

"Let me define again what I mean by 'midpoint': it is meant to show that the world is temporarily created by an aim in order to reach it. Everything else is more or less shielded. He chooses from what he finds and thinks has value toward the aim, and shapes the world. Imagine the unimaginable: having no aims at all. You would no longer have the aim of surviving, of satisfying your needs, of finding your bearings. Already in the emergence of the first life on the world you would find the aim of survival that shaped the 'view' and brought the found world into a form.

A strong aim can completely take over the human being for a period of time and structure it completely. This can be seen very well in the phenomenon of love, or when you have a task in front of you that completely engages you. Everything in one is aligned as much as possible."

"You said the aims in man are hierarchical. Do you mean that there is a command centre in the brain?"

"No, this is not existing. What I mean by this is that the more important the aims are, the higher the rank. To

achieve this, neural networks join together to form jointly acting groups,
ensembles. The hierarchy can change
constantly according to the demands
of the world."

"When and how did these networks
actually come about?"

"Human brain development begins in
the third week of pregnancy and is
largely complete only after puberty,
more than 20 years after birth.

At the time of its birth, the infant already has almost the complete number
of neurons, but only a very small part
of the nerve processes and synapses.
After birth, these multiply at breath-
taking speed and network the neurons.
They are then amplified or dissipate
again."

"By what rules?"

"It depends on what value they have
and how intensively they are used.
Experiences with the environment determine which neural networks become stronger, endure and which
don't."

"So the decisive factors are the experiences that the living being makes in the various phases?"

"The more important something is for a living being, the more it learns in this relationship. Neural networks are strengthened, redesigned or newly formed."

"Do the individual neurons only react to a specific impulse?"

"No, they can form structures with different neurons in response to different impulses, so to speak, they have multiple functions: for the respective aims, many nerve cells have the inherent ability to react to an impulse with other cells that have the same potential in milliseconds, to organize.

Take a life-threatening situation, for example. This restructures the structure at lightning speed via various activated neurons. The more life, survival is affected, the stronger the activities."

"So, no order is given from 'above'?"

"The 'command' is the perception via the senses, which triggers an impulse, which is then converted into reactions by the brain - if there is an aim for it and the impulse has the appropriate value."

"What determines the valence?"

"The aims that lie in one."

"But if you say that the life instinct is usually at the top of the hierarchy, then it would have to be found somewhere!"

"It lies in the primordial structures of living beings. From these the (psychic) life develops. "

"If one could define the aims in humans as associations of neurons, which u. a. are stimulated by stimuli to form a figure? "

"Yes. And in the same way that neurons can have multiple functions, so too are the individual aims: they can organize themselves into groups - into aims that can form action forms. At the same time, various aims are being stimulated in parallel, forming together forms. "

"Let me repeat: the impulse, the stimulus from outside or inside activates targets, these activate further neural networks and these again solution programs."

"That's the procedure," I confirmed.

"When you go from one midpoint to the other, is it like switching from one neural network to another?"

"Yes, the midpoint is made up of co-operating networks with their respective weights."

"Once again asked: Everything is subject to aims?"

"Yes, whether inorganic or organic."

"So not just the living beings?"

"Look: after the Big Bang the universe was mostly hydrogen, helium, and some lithium and beryllium. From these gases, galaxies with solar systems and planets developed under great gravitational pressure and nuclear reactions, and all the elements that we know today were formed during this time. All of this was inorganic up to a certain point in time."

"And was shaped based on aims?"

"When substances or their environment are changed, different forms and laws result.

But of course everything continues - like everything else - according to substances and laws - just according to other aims.

Everything has the aim of forming a figure according to the laws. Exactly that is also subject to everything organic. What they all have in common is that they are guided by aims. From this perspective, there is no difference between the inanimate and the animated. With the latter, only 'the aims of survival are added, which have led to increasingly complex structures."

"Why do human beings often not see that aims shape you?"

"Quite simply because they believe they are shaping themselves with her consciousness."

--- Gestalt psychology ---

GP considered. Then he said: "You probably know Max Wertheimer, who explained: 'There are connections in which what happens as a whole is not derived from how the individual pieces are and are put together, but vice versa, where what happens to a part of that whole is determined by internal structural laws of that whole.'"

I nodded. "These inner structural laws result from aims in people; they take in what he is receptive to, what is important to him, and store that as a whole. These are e.g. B. When listening to music, of course, the melody and not the individual instruments. This holistic view is an important property of all living beings."

"Wertheimer's Gestalt theory attempts to clarify the laws according to which the brain assembles elements into a whole," concluded GP.

"These are explained neither by the laws of the individual parts nor by their sum," I added. "But they are explained by the respective aim in the human being, which brings all parts with its midpoint into a structure appropriate to the aim, which is then stored in the brain.

Holistic recognition makes sense to handle situations better and faster. "

"I'll summarize it again," said *CP*. "The holistic view of the brain has the aim of being able to make quick decisions - if it were to go into all the details every time, then this delays its capture or its decision. This holistic view arises in man through experiences that he has already made in similar situations. But since these are only similar, that does not necessarily mean that they are appropriate for an aim or that it correctly indicates a lying one. "

"Correct. This usually results in a structure that you can work with without getting bogged down in the details. But it can also lead to the brain creating something wrong. This can have unpleasant consequences because one lives on with these 'facts', which can be called suggestions, which influence attitudes and behavior. It is the reason for confusion of all kinds. There are no limits to the creativity and imagination of the brain, it 'explains' everything. Especially when you don't know or recognize anything specific about something. If you notice this and it is important, the aim corrects itself."

"And you say everything in the universe is shaped by aims," *CP* was curious.

"Everything has the aim to form a figure according to the respective laws. Everything is aligned with aims. "

"Also, a lifeless stone?" *CP* smirked.

"By 'lifeless stone' you probably mean something lying around somewhere. Well, I would like to say: First, there is movement within the stone, because it consists of atoms or even smaller particle waves, which are not motionless and also run according to laws. And secondly, when this stone is moved, then it forms with its environment, the circumstances of a particular structure according to the laws. That's what I mean when I say: everything has the aim of forming a figure according to the laws."

"Could a stone form a structure even without laws?"

"How come? This is impossible because the laws are inherent in the substances. Nothing can happen without laws, because the substances are laws! "

"And so, you came to the conclusion that everything has the aim of forming a figure according to the laws."

"Right, this happens completely automatically. It is not that a stone has a consciousness that is out to obtain information. He's not alive. But since, as I said, everything runs according to laws, the aim automatically arises to create structures according to the laws of nature.

The same thing happens to the living beings, except that here the aim of survival is added. This aim shapes the human being. This is what I call mid-point or midpoint-mechanics.

Imagine a person who has no more aims. So do not eat anymore, drink, etc. What would happen to that? "

"He would probably die."

"By the way: without an aim, the placebo effect wouldn't work either. The aim here is to achieve something through medication. This creates a midpoint that pulls in everything that is useful for that aim. Of course, also experiences that were made when you were already taking any medication that helped. The logic of the brain is: If a suitable drug, which comes from a competent person, is taken against this disease, then this aim will also be fulfilled.

As a result, the previous internal structure in this relationship can change up to the fulfilment of the aim: from illness to health."

"And this is done by the brain just because it "recognized" a drug that helps in his view?"

"Yes, that is enough. Unless, for example, the consciousness (better: the perception) gives the information that there is no active ingredient in the drug or that one does not trust the person who prescribed the drug. This would severely limit or negate the effect.

--- Awareness Restriction ---

The vast majority of human reactions are unaware. Consciousness becomes only a very small part, and always when something important occurs. Then information about the consciousness is obtained. If they are relevant, the brain processes them with the midpoints.

All other reactions and behaviours take place via the general, more or less strong, attention or automatically. "

"But that must be an incredible amount of aims with their midpoints that shape the people!"

"Yes, you can say that. Just such a simple act as picking up a newspaper requires many learned aims that have been summarized and then run automatically.

Time and again, I hear that people have trouble understanding that everything is guided by aims, including themselves. I think its daily life that makes them fail to understand that sentence. Because everything is so natural, what happens. If they dig deeper, then they could see that every action, every movement is guided by aims and moves them. For example, the handle to the glass of water and drink from it. "

"Many people I've talked to actually have trouble understanding what 'aim' means," *CP* nodded. "For them, one aim is to complete a task or strive for something. But such a simple thing, such as bringing a spoon to your mouth, is not an aim for them!"

"Because it runs automatically, without paying more attention to this process. If they were to get to the bottom of this, they would come closer to the fact that every single hand movement must first be learned. The motivation was aims.

Because that's just the treachery for the realization that simple actions are taken for granted and not further think about it. Not realized that very specific aim-oriented processes are behind it."

"Yes, that's right," said *CP* thoughtfully.

"Lots of amazing achievements by people who are often based on island talents, e. B. to remember a large number of things in a limited time, to perform complex arithmetic operations in a few seconds or to learn a new language in a short time, would not be possible without an aim. This provides the structure that leads to the solution. Even artificial intelligence, which works with algorithms, does not come to a conclusion without a specified aim. "

--- thinking habits ---

I took a short break.

Then I continued: "Until the 16th century, people knew virtually no laws. Everything was determined from God's perspective. But even in our time, many are far from seeing everything controlled by aims, thinking that most things happen by themselves anyway, and still viewing consciousness as something metaphysical or something. These views have passed from generation to generation and still shape some philosophers and people who deal with these issues. Everyone else usually just takes it that way because they do not even think about it. "

"Why don't human beings often see that aims shape him?"

"Simply because they believe that they shape themself with their consciousness."

"What if they were to throw their antiquated views overboard and start thinking that consciousness is indeed just a brain information provider?"

"Most people are too caught up in their views, their habits of thought, for that. Very few of them have the aim of getting to the bottom of their processes, of dealing intensively with the course of their consciousness, as is the case with this topic. In addition, there are countless people who live in the world of esotericism and mysticism and would hurt their world if they accepted this insight. Consciousness is an essential element in the mystical worldview, shaped by a 'metaphysical' aim with its centre in them."

"You mean they create this aim themself? "

"For sure."

"The truth does not interest them, do you mean to say that," said *CP*.

They are interested in the truth," I replied, "but only in their own truth.

One can call this the drama of the blinded person. Its midpoint, the mystical world, surrounds it like a bell shielding all other views and evidence."

"Pity," said *CP*, "I find it always very exciting to hear and discuss new views."

"I feel the same way," I nodded. "Unfortunately, it is often the case that each of us has a worldview that includes a more or less strong ability to persist. Changes to settings that have become dear are reluctant to be made.

For example, branded images and ideas of the culture in which you grew up are transported from generation to generation. Only too rarely are these questioned, and if so, often with bad feelings, because they question the structures they have created: in themselves and in society. Resistance quickly builds up, trying by all means to maintain the old structures. "

"Self-knowledge doesn't seem to be an aim for many people," said CP.

"I have that impression too. Self-knowledge comes through self-observation. Who does that?"

"Funny, I enjoy watching myself and sometimes have to laugh heartily when I've seen things wrong or insisted on an erroneous point of view. By introspection, one comes closer, sees moves in ones that have not yet noticed, especially in new or critical situations.

Maybe it's also because I can accept myself and my behaviour, with the sentence, 'What happened, had to happen as it happened.' "

"I feel the same way," I confirmed. "That's why I enjoy talking to you. I've learned a lot from you already. "

"The compliment I can give back, the discussions with you are very stimulating for me.

What aims should one have?", he continued.

"I can't answer that. Everyone has their own values. I can only speak for myself here, for my aims: the most important thing for me is knowledge. I can totally immerse myself in that.

What comes to my mind right now: dissatisfaction always depends on the level of expectations."

"You mean, the decisive factor is the respective aim?"

"The more you have achieved an aim, the higher the satisfaction - and vice versa. Here you can find roots for euphoria or depression. Therefore, one should think carefully, which aims one undertakes. Are its wrong aims, for example, that cannot be achieved, then you open the door to bad mood or depression. False aims can severely burden the psyche. "

"Do you have ideals?"

--- life attitudes ---

"Not really, unless you count the truth."

"Would wealth and fame give you something?"

"If I wanted to be rich, I would have to write for people according to their expectations. So, about fairy tales, sex, crime. Those would not be desirable aims for me. I am absolutely satisfied with my life, in which I am looking for new knowledge. I wouldn't have anything from wealth, because what I want to know is primarily within me and spontaneously rises up and drives me. A lot of money would not help me in this respect.

And fame could possibly create vanity in me that does not help my actual aims, but rather hinders them. It could stop me from time to time questioning my theses and possibly insisting on them, even against legitimate objections.

There are enough examples of famous personalities. "

"You are different than most people."

"I did not aspire to that. I am the way I am, and so am I. "

"Why do people strive for greatness, for wanting to have more and more?"

"One reason will be vanity. An essential element of life is the recognition in the group, the society. The general reasons will lie in the primordial structures. "

"Therefore, people are striving for wealth, build taller buildings, clothe themselves conspicuously, show what

they have, try to achieve a high position in society?"

"I think that's the driving force. Many
people are shaped by this. "

--- fear of death ---

"Are you afraid of death?"

"I know that the midpoint of life-drive
creates this fear to drive people to
continue living. For example, it does
not matter to him whether human being is terminally ill and suffers from
horrible pain or only wishes to die.
Knowing the reason makes it easier for
me to deal with these feelings. And: If
you're dead, the reason is gone anyway, then feelings logically play no
role anymore."

"Why do many people think that death
is something very bad?"

"Because the life instinct is fooling
everyone. He is the strongest midpoint
of life. "

"But he is ultimately only an aim."

"Naturally. Therefore, for example, the suicide is also nothing wrong. Anyone who believes this merely reflects his own opinion or that of the society in which he grew up or lives. "

"And the own opinion is always relative," *CP* added.

"What do you think of near-death experiences?" he asked.

"Dying is the extinction of the organ functions of a living being, which leads to death. Death is the function setting of the neural networks in the brain.

Experiences can always only be gained through the brain. And as long as this is not dead, it is capable of producing fantasies. When the brain is dead, you do not experience anything anymore.

Near-death experiences come clearly from the brain. And the brain is not always right with what's coming out of it - that we see very clearly in the dreams."

So, one should not attach great importance to near-death experiences."

"Can you say you're always on your own trail?"

"That's not quite true, but I often spontaneously have thoughts and feelings that I follow, with which I study intensively. I research, compare, falsify and verify and try, if they help me in my desire to understand, finally to bring them understandable on paper. Hoping to get criticized if I'm wrong about a view.

In addition, there is a strange striving for perfection in the relationship that I want to answer questions that are in me to the smallest detail. These aims are sustainable in me, so even if I have answered questions, they pop up again and again and make me check to see if my answer was correct or had any errors. "

"From uncertainty?"

"Out of openness and perfection."

"So, it's not just the urge for an answer that makes you think of something, It's the urge for it?"

"Through this quest for perfection fall to me answers. And since these aims are sustainable in me, there seems to be no end to it. That's why criticism is important to me. And that's why I write.

In addition, dealing with a question always raises new questions. So, my urge to learn never actually comes to a conclusion.

Even while falling asleep and sleeping, there are suddenly thoughts or ideas, for example, about topics that I had once occupied myself with, but where I had no solution.

I then take notes for a moment, because I had the experience that if I did not write it down right away, the thoughts would have disappeared the next day. A voluntary retrieval of these target solutions is not possible for me after I wake up again. "

"All this seems to give you a lot," presumed *CP*.

"I can be completely absorbed in it", I confirmed.

Midpoint-mechanics

(A key to the psyche)

> **The function of the midpoint mechanics is generated in the psyche due to an aim to be achieved.**
>
> **This means that anything else that doesn't fit or interfere with that aim will be devalued automatically during this process.**

Midpoints are neural networks generated by aims, which then represent and execute them.

They are not rigid, but are constantly changing in terms of adapting to the environment and the inner world.

As already mentioned, other midpoints (neuron networks) that do not match are automatically reduced in value by the brain during this process.

As a rule, this is not perceived by human.

He only recognizes what the midpoints (aims) in the brain show him.

Midpoints consist of neurons distributed far and wide across the brain, which involve many areas and form a network that serves to form attitudes, actions, ideas

and especially feelings

to create.

Feelings form in order to be able to react quickly in similar situations.

In addition, they develop fine adjustments for situations and tasks.

And last but not least, they are guardians of survival.

Depending on the flexibility of the respective brain, there are always new networks in addition to the existing ones, which are formed, i.e. by adapting to the outside or inside world (lightning-fast or gradually).

Other midpoints are changed or closed for these reasons.

While everything in the universe is shaped by aims who "don't care" about the consequences of structure, with living beings the aim of preservation is added (to survive).

This takes place in the brain through networks of neurons, glial cells and synapses, which I call "midpoints". Depending on the type and individual, the living beings are shaped by them.

As a general knitting pattern, the example of how to learn to ride a bike:

In the beginning there is the aim. This creates a neural network in the brain to reach it.

Balance, muscles, tendons, posture, mental processes, etc. are developed as sub-aims in the required form, coordinated with one another and temporarily stored.

So gradually the skills are improved; you learn from your mistakes.

This is all done by the neural networks formed by the aim of cycling and then further evolving to expand body-psyche coordination and fine-tune adjustments.

The network at the beginning (the midpoint of cycling) has now become far-reaching interdependencies. Which,

> when the respective sub-aims
> have been achieved, are
> stored permanently and be-
> come an automatic behaviour
> that is activated when you
> get back on the bike.

Midpoints are thus created by aims and are their tools.

Neural networks connect areas of the brain such as: frontal lobe, cerebral cortex, cerebellum, limbic system, amygdala, language midpoint, visual cortex, hearing center, taste center, etc., and access memory content and everything that goes with it.

There is also a constant exchange of information with the autonomic nervous system (plus the somatic nervous system) and the enteric nervous system (which is also called the 'abdominal brain').

Midpoints act in such a way that they allow everything that

could help to achieve or maintain their structure - the aim - and do not take everything else into account as far as possible.

This usually continues unconsciously.

Anyone who becomes aware of this mechanism also understands a lot about how their own psyche works.

In general, the midpoints play the concert of life with one another; many processes take place at the same time.

In extreme cases, however, one midpoint can greatly reduce all the others so that only this midpoint shapes people, for example in phases of panic, ecstasy or when one is about to achieve maximum performance.

But even in the spectrum between normal and extreme, all midpoints act in such a way that they limit or strengthen others in value.

Another reason why it is so difficult to explain the midpoint mechanics to other people is that they are always on some aim without really realizing it. They cannot or do not see their psychological processes.

What is even less perceived is that a lot no longer plays a role due to the respective aim.

One should perhaps have had the experience that one's view of the world can change in fractions of a second in order to understand it better.

I formed the term "midpoint-mechanics" in order not to always use neural-network-laws. It makes clearer in a more memorable way that a neural network mechanically reduces or strengthens others in value, depending, as I said, whether they are unsuitable or suitable for the current midpoint.

And one more hint:

Most explanations of how the brain works boil down to certain areas being activated and responding to stimuli.

But never just one area reacts; rather a neuron network (which connects different sub-areas via synapses) is always activated by the stimuli, which communicates with others. Because of course not the whole area is used, but only a part, which is usually not strictly limited, but is dependent on the other neuron network.

You could compare it to preparing a meal:

Knowledge plays an important role. In other words, what you need in what quantity, which procedure must be followed, what the hands or devices have to do, what

amount of energy is re-
quired, whether the taste is
right, etc. All of this
works together in the right
amount and forms that Meal.

Applied to the work of the
brain to achieve an aim,
this means that each brain
area contributes a limited
part that activates the responsible neural network in
order to come to a successful conclusion.

Just as the ingredients etc.
are not used without re-
striction, so is the brain.
Here a neural network is in
charge, there the recipe.

Perhaps the terms "selective attention" and "flow" will help you understand better. In the first, only certain information that fits an aim is perceived from a large number of pieces of information. With the second one is in a flow that is only determined by one aim and does not allow anything else, i.e. is not disturbed by anything.

Both also apply to the midpoint-mechanics. Here, however, there is also the reference to the strict regularity with which perception is restricted. This means that the brain only perceives what is essential for the respective aim or aims. Everything else is absolutely not noticed and is virtually non-existent.

So, nothing is rated negatively or suppressed (accordingly, it does not trigger any reactions). So, the process is not disturbed by anything; one only lives in the world of the respective aim.

Without the midpoint mechanics, the brain would plunge into chaos because

aims could no longer be pursued permanently.

As I said, it is relatively seldom that people are shaped by only one midpoint. As a rule, many processes take place at the same time, all of which run according to the midpoint-mechanics and, depending on their value, are more or less important for other aims. This creates for example certain clusters that execute processes together.

In one sentence:

The more the brain pursues an aim, the less there will be other aims that do not contribute to it can, perceived or can work.

This is presented again in great detail in the **conversation about the midpoint mechanics at the end of this book.**

In this context, the experiment with a large number of people with a video of 75 seconds duration that the scientists Simons and Chabris carried out and called it "gorillas in our midst" is perhaps also interesting:

The film shows two teams with three players each, one wearing white and the other black T-shirts. The members of each team play a normal orange basketball by throwing or dribbling. After 44 to 48 seconds, something unexpected happens: a smaller person, completely wrapped in a gorilla costume, walks across the screen in the same way as the players. During these unexpected events, the basketball players unwaveringly continue their actions.

Before the test subjects see a video, they are given the task of either concentrating on the team in white or on the team in black and counting all rallies of the observed team in their heads or counting the thrown and dribbled rallies separately. After the test subjects have seen the video and completed their observation task, they are asked to write down their num-

bers. Then you ask them if (a) they noticed something unusual while counting, (b) if they noticed anything other than the six players, if someone else appeared in the video, finally: (c) Do you have a gorilla see going through the picture?

About half of the subjects did not notice the gorilla.

My interpretation of this: The given aims (the midpoints) did not allow everything else (including the gorilla) to be perceived.

On the basis of this experiment one can clearly see how a midpoint - here the task - works.

And one more note: wizards and hypnotists all work with the midpoint-mechanics.

Finally:

Who hasn't wondered why people can do something that goes far

**Here, too, the midpoint mechanism
is the key to understanding it.**

Because with it you can make all extreme behaviours clear.

Two small examples for better understanding:

▸ You are talking to someone about a topic (so you are in the midpoint of it). Suddenly you have the feeling that the other person is insulting you.

This can result in a new midpoint emerging,

122

which weakens the pre-
vious one.

▸ You are on your way
to work and thinking
about the tasks ahead
of you.

Suddenly you witness a
robbery and are now in
this midpoint (with
your mind).

If you later look back
at your altered state,
you will find that the
raid suddenly eliminat-
ed all previous
thoughts. This new mid-
point has reduced eve-
rything else to zero.

Theorem:

> ## The midpoint is the structure that makes an aim out of you.

Appendix

> **Non-perception due to the midpoint - mechanism**
>
> **vs. repression**
>
> "If you say: 'A midpoint prevents you from perceiving something', then you get to the point much more accurately

124

than if you say: 'You have repressed something'."

"I understood it like this," CP summed up: "An aim has to be achieved. To do this, a certain structure is needed. This is created from what is relevant to it, everything else is ignored. If something is disturbing, its value is reduced, so it has much less influence on the person."

I nodded. "This reduction of the other values does not happen intentionally, but mechanically. It is a lawful process. That is why I called it 'midpoint - mechanism'.

An example: On March 24, 2015, a pilot committed suicide in a passenger plane. He steered the plane into a rock massif. He took all 150 passengers with him to their deaths.

What was going on in this person's head?

The answer is provided by the midpoint - mechanism: the aim of taking one's own life reduced the value of all other midpoints (aims) or reduced them to zero; the impending collision with the mountains, the people who were on board and had to die with him, their relatives who had to suffer the loss, etc.

On the one hand, it is frightening what midpoints can do, including the terrible atrocities of the Nazi regime or inhumane acts that virtually all peoples committed."

"Or what individual people did to others," added CP.

"Yes. On the other hand, it is beautiful what midpoints can do.

For example, love, standing up for people or other living beings.

"What can you do to escape a negative focus, not to be a slave to it and to expand your perception?"

"In quiet moments, look closely at it and ask yourself what aim is behind it.

Then: create a counter-aim and link it to the midpoint. That means: create a new aim that is activated every time the impulse tries to provoke negative behaviour, and thus dampens and regulates it, influencing your own behaviour more and more.

Emotional sensations

(Definition and Description)

Since the emergence of the first organisms around 3.5 billion years ago, feelings have accompanied life and especially survival.

Feelings arise in humans - like cognitive experiences - due to aims in the brain and are stored in the respective neural networks.

They guide people. In addition to cognition, feeling is the other pillar that controls people.

Everything that a person has experienced or has experienced is accompanied by feelings that are stored.

This means that people's feelings very often play a more dominant role than their cognition.

As I said: Emotions are formed because of aims. They range from fine-tuning (to do something precisely) to violent urges (when the brain judges it to be of the utmost importance) and are often stronger than reason; it's hard to resist them - as everyone knows. They can blind you completely.

The midpoints create a world aligned with the target. This generates corresponding feelings that more or less urge to satisfy the aim. Feelings are therefore dependent on the aims in the brain.

If you have wrong aims in yourself, wrong, mostly unhealthy feelings are also generated.

Feelings can control people very well. Therefore, everything he does, experiences etc. is accompanied by it.

It is much more economical to summarize important situations in feelings, which should later help in similar states to evaluate them more quickly than if the brain were to store all the details of what was in front of a person and act on the basis of this image.

Many variable feelings can overlap and form a pattern that has the character of a request in similar situations.

Regarding wrong aims: In daily life one is dependent on one's cognitions. These show us the world through the aims in the brain. This then also affects the feelings as a result: They are not properly attuned to the world with regard to wrong aims. if e.g. For example, if your gut feeling says you should decide this or that one way or the other, then you can often register later that you made the wrong decision.

But the feelings are often right. So, it's not that easy to spot false feelings. But if something very important is at stake, then it would be good to review what has been said above and turn on the thinking. At the same time, this activates the awareness that what the feelings want can be looked at more closely with strengthened senses. And this gives the brain information from its feelings and thinking and thus the possibility to revise its decision.

Again, and again you experience feelings that tell you 100% that this or

that is absolutely right and in order
and want to lead you there - sometimes with strong urges. However, if
you are not an expert in the field (but
also sometimes if you are an expert),
you should perhaps question these
feelings critically. Because the less you
know about something, the more your
feelings can creatively fool you.

The brain makes its own, sometimes
erroneous, interpretations, thereby
misleading humans.

Depending on the value of the aim,
feelings can be very strong. Especially
when an essential value has to be giv-
en up. For example, when you're
grieving. Here an old aim has to give
way to a new one, namely the realization that something you loved is no
longer there. The old aim creates the
tears, the pain because it can no longer be reached.

So, when you're sad, going through
the range of emotions, it's always because of an aim that can no longer be
reached. This works until you come to
terms with it.

Psyche

▶ Where is the psyche located?

In the brain.

▶ What is their job?

It strives to carry out the aims located in the respective living being. The psyche serves to preserve life by adapting to the environment, e.g. by feeling, thinking, learning.

▶ How does it work?

Through aims that have created neural network connections (midpoints).

The psyche consists of the aims that are or form in the human brain and move it with the resulting midpoints, consciously and unconsciously.

With regard to the activity, which depends on the state and course of the outside world and the condition of the inner states, there are the midpoints acting in the foreground or background and currently passive ones (e.g. midpoints in a new environment are superficially active, parallel to this, social behaviours are running in the background, and passive aims are those that are currently satisfied or not needed).

The midpoints were and are initially generated by aims and represent them. That is, if a neural network is stimulated, the aim is activated.

Depending on the demands of life, there are always new aims that create the midpoints.

(The processes of learning or unlearning take place in the synapses of the neurons).

Midpoints can increase or decrease in value depending on when and how often they are used. If they are no longer needed, they weaken and usually disappear.

Psychic phenomena or functions, i.e., acts, states, patterns, experiences, are generally the effects of neuron networks that interact with other midpoints and generate feelings in parallel.

Depending on the aims, the midpoints are networked with one another, can form clusters (an association for certain processes) and, as a rule, always learn something new.

In this way, the psyche in the brain remains flexible and adaptable.

The psyche is not to be equated with the soul because supernatural elements are believed to exist here.

Of course, faith can also be at the midpoints of the psyche, affecting other neuronal networks.

This is particularly true of the religious, mystical themes that, in the person concerned, can evoke a self-fulfilling prophecy through the perspective those results, altering his psyche.

Mental satisfaction and balance are shown when the midpoints harmonize with each other.

More or less imbalance results for example, if aims with their midpoints influence others negatively in their function beyond what is healthy. Or cannot be achieved. This can occur due to expectations that are too high.

Here one could say: Satisfaction generally depends on the level of expectation.

So, if you are dissatisfied, you should look for the aims - and possibly modify them. (Change them or replace them with another aim).

Sleep and dreams create different patterns in the psyche because brain functions then work differently.

And again, the comment on the mind:

Was asked once:

▶ **How does the mind get into the machine (here: the human body)?**

Reply:

▶ **It is part of the brain from birth. It just needs to evolve, like everything else.**

Mind and brain are mutually dependent in humans.

Mind are structures that form through aims.

THE SELF

The SELF is a relatively small, but - in terms of its values - an essential part in the human brain - and also acts from this.

Among other things, it decides through control efforts with - over its respective midpoints, which have formed from its aims.

It is initially formed from feelings: what I like, what I don't like. Over time, this changes to: I want that, I don't want that. And the SELF forms itself accordingly. The aims are correspondingly stored in the brain and work unconsciously or consciously.

Depending on the level of development, they are supplemented with cognitive personal aims.

That SELF can control areas of the psyche up to certain

limit thresholds and, if necessary, influence them more or less with his will. So, overcome other aims in his psyche via the midpoint-mechanics.

But the stronger other feelings (as aims) are, the more difficult it becomes.

In general: The more the feelings have power in the aims, the more difficult it is for the mind.

This has to be explained - not feelings! These run according to the laws inherent in them, which can make it difficult for the mind to influence.

This will also have to do with the fact that people have developed through feelings in the course of their evolution - the mind only much later.

Also for this reason - and because it is much easier than using the mind - feeling is often preferred.

> **The SELF is also a postulated instance in Freud's psychoanalysis, which is equated with consciousness.**
>
> **Now, however, consciousness is merely a function that is intended to provide the aims in the brain with more precise information with increased senses, since they can make adequate decisions.**
>
> **Therefore, Freud's abovementioned ego invention makes no sense.**
>
> # In one sentence: consciousness is not the self!

The SELF, that is, what you mean, what you are yourself, as I said, is formed from the feelings of human being, from his mental state. The beginning is around the end of the 2nd year of life.

Here personal aims gradually emerge.

One more word about the SELF-ideal:

This is how you would like to be your-self. And, as you might think, others should see you.

It can harm you by setting wrong
aims.

How to perceive the
world
(Definition and explanation)

One can look at the world as
a fixed entity that is the
same from every point of
view.
This is called outside-in
theory.

However, one can also see
the world in such a way that
different creatures see it
differently in terms of
their aims.
This is what I call the

inside-out theory.

There, as here, the sensors
receive stimuli from the
outside world. A few impulses are enough to get an
idea.

In contrast to the outside-
in theory, however, the
world is created by the respective living beings according to their aims:
The sensors send the recorded information to the neural
networks. If it is deter-
mined there that the world
they perceive differs from
that stored in the mid-
points, they may process
their view of the world.

This process can be followed immediately:

The world that living beings, including humans, perceive is one that results from **their aims that neural networks have built up.** (Just as after conception the body builds itself according to inherited aims, so does the psyche: **these aims create neural networks** in order to be reached.)

According to these, the sensors see the world. As soon as the inner world differs from the outer world, the neural networks may change their structures.

This is how man perceives
the world according to his
psychic aims.

!! The world that shows itself to us is of course there first, but what people absorb from it is decided by the brain according to its aims. !!

Even if you want to record everything that is around you, it always remains a matter of the limits of our senses and brain.

Wikipedia (definition): In living beings, perception is the process and the subjective result of information acquisition (reception) and processing of stimuli from the environment and from the body. This happens through unconscious (and sometimes conscious in humans) filtering and merging of partial information into subjectively meaningful overall impressions. These are also called precepts and are continuously compared with stored ideas (constructs and schemes).

► According to this definition, there would be the world first, which is created by filtering and merging partial information into subjectively meaningful overall impressions in living beings.

This raises the question: According to which directives are the filtering and merging of partial information carried out?

The answer could only be: Through the aims in the brain, which are focused by means of the sensors, which are focused by its values (aims) (i.e. where the attention should be directed).

► So, I think it's the other way around: that first the brain (the midpoints) has an approximate expectation about the world according to its aims. Then this is perceived by the senses selected in this way. Once this is done, inequalities in these two worlds (expec-

tation and fact) are corrected by the brain in milliseconds when it feels right according to its aims.

First of all, you always see the world according to your habits, expectations, and ideas that are stored in your brain about aims. If it recognizes (because it is valuable) that it deviates from it, then the perception is adjusted accordingly. Aims learn or form a new – again initially according to the aims that one has inherited or learned, because only through them can one originally perceive the world.

There is no world as it actually and always is, but only one from the perspective of the respective observer.

Therefore, we do not see the world as it appears to be in front of us (that is, the same for everyone), but one that the brain shows us based on its aims.

Since every person has their own characteristic aims, they also see their own world, to which they react individually.

(By the way, since each species has its specific aims, the world sees them similarly).

Again: People can only perceive the world from the perspective of the respective observer.

For clarification:

The world that we see is of course still there, even if we are no longer there. However, it would change according to the respective perception by other beings who are different from us.

Because there is no such thing as a world that is always the same.

What stays forever - no matter what perspective you look at it from - is that <u>identical sub-</u>

> stances under identical condi-
> tions always show identical re-
> sults.

Summarized:

> Human beings see the world from their point of view. This results from the aims of the respective person. Namely from his currently active ones or especially from those currently additionally stimulated.
>
> ▶ The active aims shape the world into a structure that is needed to achieve them.
>
> ▶ Depending on the value of the stimuli that are now activated, further aims are awakened, which additionally structure the view.
>
> ▶ So, there is ultimately no identical world that everyone sees the same, but many different, from the point of view of the respective aims.

And: intellect means to perceive something precisely, i.e. to understand it.

You can only grasp what you have a system for.

(If one encounters something absolutely new, then of course one can also take in and grasp it - but, as I said, only according to one's predispositions aims). In this way, the new from the environment and inner field of the human being, from the brain, becomes his predispositions adjusted accordingly.

So, you absorb the world first through the aims in yourself and then with the aligned senses – in that order.

The senses are constantly confronted with unfiltered stimuli (approx. 11 million bits per second), but they do not simply represent the world in front of us 1:1, but the brain selects them with its aims, which align the senses in such a way that they only perceive the information that fits the aims of the brain because it is important.

These million bits are not there to depict the environment precisely for us, but to compare the structures that arise after selection through our aims with those stored in the brain and, if necessary, to correct them by learning (changing synapses).

In general, then, man has his hereditary world in the head brain, the autonomic nervous system (plus the somatic nervous system) and the abdominal brain (enteric nervous system), along with those who have experiences and learning were built in him.

This is the reason why we each perceive the world differently and possibly wrongly; because we weren't in the right midpoints. (Wrong in relation hung that we have disadvantages, e.g., not respond appropriately.)

And since the selection by the aims also influences the storage of experiences in the brain, this can lead to incorrect information.

A little excursion to objectivity:

How do animals, bacteria and viruses perceive the world?

And who sees the world more correctly?

Of course, people will say: the world
ultimately looks the way we see it.

Anyone who says you can only see the
world from a human perspective is
definitely **right**.

Anyone who believes that this is being
said about a basic world that is eternal
and unchangeable is certainly **wrong**.

Because the world is basically **not** in
an eternally identical state (because
processes are constantly taking place
on all levels).

A little incentive to think:

What should the brain also perceive
when you say you see it for what it is?

The answer is only possible in relation
to aims that reside in oneself - in the
brain.

And: people's perception is limited. As
for hearing and seeing with the respective bandwidth. Or e.g., the inabil-

ity to perceive radioactivity, mag-
netism, ultrasound, etc.

**There is no world that is the same
and unchangeable from every perspective.**

Summarized:

Viewed from living beings, the world is subjective.

Recorded by an apparatus - regardless of the perspective - it is always objective.

But this does not mean: forever fixed and immutable, because the world is constantly changing.

Only the laws according to which substances move are eternal.

And all perspectives of the macro- or micro world result in the sentences:

- **Identical substances under identical circumstances always give identical results.**

● The reason for this is that everything is subject to unchangeable laws.
● If you change substances or circumstances, then other laws also appear.

If you turn 180 degrees in a strange environment, it takes milliseconds before you consciously perceive what is in front of you.

This attaches to the brain: First, the general perception occurs according to its expectations. (If there are no specific ones, it looks for similarities). Depending on the extent to which this does not match what is in front of you, it is corrected if it is relevant.

The aim of orientation requires data from the senses to clarify whether and to what extent the world shown by the brain may deviate from reality in order to be able to adapt. This takes milliseconds. (The aim of orientation is a central aim in living beings).

Recognition also takes place through aims; one recognizes what was stored in the brain. This is also where the

153

reason for confusion can be found (because the brain searches for similarities).

The selected stimuli may change existing neuronal networks in the brain or generate new ones if aims (midpoints) in the psyche consider this to be important. If the stimuli show more or less strong differences from what has been stored up to now, it is adjusted.

By means of the senses, which send information to the brain via attention, this is always up to date - if the aims of perception are not restricted too much by certain (rigid) midpoints.

Without new information from the senses, the brain is virtually blind - and only acts according to the previous information it had stored - as happens in a dream.

> **First you see the world that you last saved in yourself. If the senses recognize this differently, the storage changes - if the brain decides, this is important.**

> **> E.g., when a landscape that has been seen fleetingly but**

assessed as irrelevant is seen by the senses. (The brain stays with its vision). <

> It is different when, for example, you wake up from sleep and the world saved before going to bed has changed. At first you see - expected - the world after the routine storage. But if the senses send other stimuli, then the brain will include them in its vision, because it is usually important in order to be able to deal with the immediate world.
The evaluation and any change take place very quickly (as I said: in milliseconds). <

> This is also how it happens in dreams: the senses, which are directed inward due to sleep, take the stimuli of the dream world as facts that the brain - and consequently we - take as reality due to its changed structure during sleep. <

Regarding knowledge, individual things are not important. It all depends on the aim. If this is to look at details, only then will these be particularly perceived. But when it comes to saving the overall impression, then you perceive it as a whole.

The perception of music can serve as an example: You perceive the whole and not the individual instruments, because that is not the aim. (The whole thing is to perceive the feeling of music). The perception of individual devices would cloud the perception, because it could lead to other central points and be distracted.

This is exactly how you absorb everything in daily life from your aims. And that's how you see the world.

If something is no longer correct (e.g., something dangerous appears) then a target is activated in order to perceive it specifically. This suddenly puts you in a different focus. This is also recorded holistically and creates a different pattern in the brain.

Again: How and with what a room is filled is initially not important as long as one is aiming to perceive this room.

156

Only when you look more closely through other aims do they gain value.

Conclusion: the brain always absorbs holistically. The stimulated aims can change the topics quickly.

Thinking

The attitude that humans always act with their intellect first leads them away from answering the question:

"What are the most basic mechanisms in the brain that enable human thought?"

Because humans are always controlled first by the emotional aims within them. (Just as it was at the time of the first life, which arose from matter and wanted to survive.

This method (the process) has been preserved to this day.

The intellect, which came later, has the task of looking at the questions in a more differentiated way.

This means: It is not the intellect that leads people in the first place, but their feelings.

The reversal of this sentence is based solely on the aim of hubris: to separate people from other living beings that are controlled by feelings - and thereby buy their (will) "freedom".

There is "flying" and "searching" thinking. While the first is more of a scanning, the second is intensively (cognitively) concerned with aims within oneself:

(Then there is the ancient behavior pattern, which is similar to a pecking bird that takes in the environment in order to be able to react quickly in the event of danger.

This allows the brain of the Human centers are stimulated, which leads to increased attention and influences the psyche through the center mechanism.

The unintentional thinking has the consequence that topics are stimulated and possibly activate midpoint that distract one from the current activity.

Mindfulness exercises and meditation can help against the impact of the constant chattering of thoughts.

In general, this continuous polling is useful; but it can also be too much.)

The cognitive thinking is an interplay about an aim (a question or an issue): between the general attention, or consciousness (increased perception of the information) and the mind in the brain.

Thinking always means: an impulse that triggers concentration on a topic, an aim, and what then occurs to the questions asked by the brain – its huge organic networks.

Because everything that human has inherited and experienced is found within himself – in whatever form.

It intensifies the consciousness (the sensors). This strengthens the mind to collect information on this.

This activates neural networks (mid-points), prompting the mind to look here for experiences or similarities on the subject.

Results that come particularly close to the aim become conscious through increased attention and steer the mind in this direction.

This process of thinking: midpoints > consciousness > midpoints goes on until you have a coherent feeling, you can't get any further or it is replaced by another topic.

The brain compares and offers alternatives.

It makes suggestions, anticipates them and anticipates results - the

**consciousness lives them and re-
turns the information to the brain**.

This is the process of thinking.

**And by the way: Concentrated
thinking is always conscious.**

Why can hardly a person see that his
brain (which of course also includes
the SELF with its aims and will) controls it?

Answer: Because the feeling tells him
something else; namely, that **he determines everything** with his will.

Feelings are control mechanisms that
can have a great deal of power and
persuasion over people.

His feeling tells him that he controls
himself, with his consciousness - because that is the experience of the
feelings and is not questioned.

Rational explanations such as: everything is decided by the brain or there
is no "free" will usually have almost no
influence. Because this would limit the
pleasant feeling of freedom.

However, if one or the other asks himself whether this feeling is correct, that he has the free will to decide with his SELF or his consciousness, then the brain will still say "yes". Because there are often quick and not well-thought-out answers. It is simply too difficult for him to switch on the frontal lobe more intensively and thereby try to confirm or refute this feeling.

In addition, there may be the fear that one actually has no free will, and that the view of making decisions exclusively with one's (metaphysical) consciousness is nothing more than imagination.

So, if you want to get to the bottom of thinking, the brain, especially the frontal lobe, has to deal with it in detail.

This is done very well through self-observation.

> • So, once again the process in detail: You want to know something (for example a solution to a problem, how you can realize an idea, why something happened, etc.)

- This creates an aim each time.

- This activates the brain searching through the neural networks (the midpoints) for what might match. It makes suggestions or makes decisions. So, change the question with appropriate information.

- If that is not enough, this process continues.

One becomes more or less aware of what has been found. E.g. through an intuition, through pictures, schemes, designs, feelings.

As a result, information - from outside and inside - is taken in by the enhanced senses, which the consciousness then reflects back to the brain, which can then create a modified answer - these solutions may accept or reject and then, if necessary, search further. Until, as a rule, you get the feeling that what you wanted to know has been adequately answered.

A note on consciousness: anyone who believes that human

decides all this with his consciousness would have to explain where the information that consciousness needs to make decisions comes from. And he won't bother to say they come from the brain. As a result, consciousness must also have access to the brain and find out what is right for the decision. This would be a task that would take a lot of time every time because the amount of information in the brain is huge. Consciousness would have to have the entire brain under control. So, everything you have learned, what you have inherited, what has changed in the meantime, etc. And a consciousness of this kind would then have to select according to the decision, put it together and create a solution.

This kind of consciousness is nowhere to be found, let alone proven.

Summary of steps:

▶ A question appears.

▶ Where does it come from?

▶ Out of the brain! – And here from an aim that is to be achieved (to answer the question). Impulses from the outside world also pass through the brain first.

▶ Whenever a question arises, the brain first gives an answer – never consciousness.

▶ Even if the SELF gives the answer, it comes from the brain – because the SELF with its aims is in the brain.

▶ If something is important, you become aware of it.

▶ The consciousness absorbs information for the brain with enhanced senses.

▶ Then further questions may arise.

▶ This goes back and forth until the brain has made the decision that the aim has more or less been achieved. This is usually also realized in the end.

▶ As a result, people believe that they themselves have made this decision with their consciousness.

Most people prefer to make decisions based on their feelings rather than thinking. Because it is easier and far less stressful.
But this does not lead to more clarity!

Finally, a remark on Descartes' sentence: "I think, therefore I am."
I would like to add: "I am because I think."

GUT FEELING

For many people, gut feeling is a kind of intuition or sixth sense.

But it is certainly not wrong to understand the real reason that triggers the gut feeling: It is based on similar experiences in the past or is innate with similarities in these situations.

Similar experiences in other situations can be useful, but are usually not congruent.

You always experience feelings that tell you one hundred percent that this or that is absolutely correct and in order and that urge you to make this decision.

If you ultimately decide against the feeling, you can get a bad gut feeling.

However, if you are not an expert in the field (but also sometimes if you are an expert), you should critically question these feelings. Because the less you know about a thing, the more they can creatively pretend.

If e.g., the gut feeling says, this or that should be decided one way or the other, then you can often register later that you made a wrong decision.

Of course, the feelings are often right. Because the same experiences with regard to similar events usually lead to corresponding results.

So, it is not so easy to discover wrong feelings.

If, however, something very important is involved, then it would be good to look back at what has been said above and turn on your thinking. In this way, one activates the consciousness at the same time, which can take a closer look at what the feelings want with intensified senses. And this gives the brain the opportunity to revise its decision with this information.

Info:

The abdominal brain - enteric nervous system (ENS) - consists of around 100 to 200 million nerve cells.

In comparison: the head brain consists of around 100 billion nerve cells - a thousand times as many.

The brains communicate with each other: 90% from the stomach to the brain and 10% vice versa.

> If a decision is pending, the brain looks
> for similar situations and checks the
> sensation for them. (In the head and
> abdominal brain.)

First impression

The first impression is made by feeling. At first glance, it projects everything into the object that is similar to it.

Therefore, you should not rely on it one hundred percent. This is sometimes negative because one starts from false subjective assumptions.

It is better to keep an open mind in order to be able to correct the first impression.

The next impressions may already be different. But often the first impression is consolidated and directly determines the view and one's own behaviour towards the object from this perspective.

It particularly determines the emotional attitudes and sees e.g. another person from this angle. A change is often difficult, also because the brain has already stored it in this form.

The factual circumstances are different. Firstly, there are usually not that many feelings involved here, and secondly, if there are new circumstances, you have to adapt to them. This is more a task of the frontal lobe.

Wrong aims

(The Traps)

(Conversation about)

With the topics:

> The dark side
> Life aims
> Frame

"You spoke of 'fake aims'. How would you define that? " CP asks.

"Wrong aims are behaviours that harm you (and possibly others)", I answer. "First of all, aims are the essence of the universe. More precisely, everything wants to form a figure - a structure - according to the laws. "

"So, it is with the human beings?"

"Of course, the human being is not outside the universe - accordingly, he is also subject to this principle, runs according to aims:

The inorganic is governed by laws (which may be called as aims).
The organic as well. But here are the aims of survival, which complicate the simple processes and allow more laws to come into play.

Now there are healthy and unhealthy aims.
The latter I call 'false aims'.
If you go into this, you will not see the consequences via the midpoint-mechanics if possible.
Anything that could harm them is lowered in value, to a level that is less noticed or completely eliminated.
That way they can shape one more or less - and they act accordingly unhealthily."

"Could you give an example of wrong aims?"

"Well - about an addiction. If you are affected by this, many healthy aims can often only work in a limited way. "

"Do you like to say what your wrong aims are?"

"My personal? For example, anything that does not fit my frame. "

I thought. "It's like this: Not everything that rises emotionally or mentally comes to mind is right, so healthy."

"You do not trust your feeling?"

"The more experience I have in a field, the more I trust my feelings."

"So, you could set the rule: the more experience one has in an area, the more one can trust one's feelings when making decisions - and vice versa?"

I nodded in agreement. "Human are born into a society and accept their aims ..."

"You mean, for the reason just mentioned, some of those aims might be wrong?" CP interrupted.

"For sure. Since they shape a human being, he is brought into a certain structure by them, he often cannot see the negative part of it, or, if he does, it's hard to change because they have a tough persistence effect. They are intrinsic and often authoritarian.

The brain works with similarities - so human also react similarly in later life in similar situations - and has difficulty escaping this trap if these reactions have become unhealthy over time.
For example, because it makes it easier to adapt to a changed world or new knowledge. You could possibly change it by understanding the reason and the process."

I thought for a moment. "To get back to the nature of the aims: how aims work, how to be governed by them, for example in unusual situations, you notice when you react sometimes, even though you did not want to react."

CP nodded. "You once defined it like that: **'The midpoint is the shape that makes an aim of one'**."

"Yes, in this case the wrong target. The midpoint structures the perception of the outer world and that of oneself. He chooses out of what he finds and what he thinks has value for the aim. Everything else is reduced in value. The aim gives shape to the world. This can go so far that you cannot see things as they were, because they are totally re-evaluated. The midpoint can be like a sorcerer, changing everything with lightning speed. This is how a new world is created. This gives rise to freedom, that is to say, one does not perceive much, or only perceives it marginally. At the same time, however, one is also trapped in the midpoint and no longer sees many things. It only comes to the fore, which is important. Everything else, passes' so to speak. "

"The midpoints then takes over the direction, makes the human beings?"

"Yes. Aims are the key factors. "Everything has the aim of forming a figure according to the laws. Whatever one questions, analyses or researches on the causes: Without exception, you will find aims that have been structured according to the respective midpoints.

--- the dark site ---

I was silent for a while. Then I continued, "Regarding finding the wrong targets: However, sometimes it can be very hard to figure out what aims are behind a behaviour. Especially, when

they belong to the dark side of human.
"

"Under 'dark side' do you understand what exactly?"

"Anything that is difficult or impossible to reconcile with your own conscience and that could hurt your self-esteem.

These aims can be very well camouflaged. In some cases, if you want to track them down, you need to be extremely honest with yourself. And this is often painful because the beautiful image you have of yourself becomes uncomfortable and sometimes very embarrassing. Man wants to keep his previous positive self-image as possible. "

"Self-knowledge can be so difficult."

"Yes, and the harder you go deeper into your dark layers, the harder it becomes."

--- life aims ---

"What should one, generally speaking, aspire to?" He changed the subject.

"Health and sufficient means to life."

"That sounds relatively modest."

"It's healthy to be modest. And I think you should not overdo your aims, because aims that are not achievable are always wrong aims. "

"With what effects?"
"If you can run the risk of being permanently frustrated by constantly failing to reach an impossible aim, it can lead to depression."

"So, you should set your aims realistic."

"Important aims are set in childhood. If the parents come up with the idea of demanding something from their child for their life that cannot possibly be achieved, also from their later structure, then you plant a wrong aim in people that can stress them to the end of their lives. Such aims are often set in the unconscious and are difficult to uncover.

In any case, since satisfaction depends on the level of expectation, one should not set too high or hard to achieve aims. Because that's very likely to set your own dissatisfaction. "

"You say the less an aim is achieved, the more dissatisfaction can grow."

I nodded. "A wrong aim is also to try to change things of the past, for example, because you made mistakes.
Anyone who does not accept the past – and this includes the most recent, that is, what has just happened - has one false aim: namely, the assumption that the world should have been so, that it should have happened the way it is had introduced himself. "

"Acceptance means only fighting not against the past, but the future, and that includes the youngest, trying to shape things differently, right?"

"That's what I mean. Otherwise, energy is wasted unnecessarily. "

"So, a wrong target is also, if not what has hoped, and you are angry at it, complains about the fate? So, is anger at the world, non-acceptance always a mistake?"

"Naturally."

"For the terminally ill, is life - staying alive - a wrong destination?"

"Yes, that will torment him, as long as his aim is not death."

"So long as he cannot let go of life?" "Yes, to be left by the old aim."

I thought for a moment and then I said, "Even if I repeat myself: What happened, had to happen, as it happened.

Any unhealthy thing you are aiming for is wrong aims. And you have the merciless freedom to pursue them - and to bear the consequences.

A good example of wrong aims are thoughts and feelings that fool you into coming from God or a higher mystical instance. Because there is neither God nor a higher mystical entity. "

"So, you should see what targets are in one, have taken root?"

"It's very important to recognize yourself. As I said, this includes the belief that there is a God. Perhaps this could be helped by dealing with its primordial structures.

Or that life, generally speaking, makes no sense. "

"General?"

"By this I mean that you cannot make this statement in general, because the meaning of life is to live and to produce offspring (because it lies in the primordial structures). It may well apply to a limited extent that life no longer has any meaning if you are terminally ill and suffer excruciating pain.

Well, in any case, false aims in humans can have catastrophic consequences - for humans themselves and for their fellow human beings. "

"That includes superstition?"

"Surely. Superstition - that is to say, in spite of all the contradictory proofs - is a false aim that makes people see the world wrong. "

"Maybe human wants to see the world like that - although this view is not the right one?"

"I could imagine that. Humans like to fade out with the midpoint-mechanics, which could affect his beliefs.

There are also people who believe that everything in or out of them is right and healthy - and perhaps believe that a higher authority - such as God - has set it up that way.

That's blind. Blinded by a wrong target that may even fool you, you are perfect in yourself.

This is part of the area of complacency; to see everything as positive as possible - and thereby to feel satisfied.

Of course, those who are designed in this way do not work on their own, do not question parts of themselves - and thus always make the same mistakes. And can be a danger to themselves and others because these people often do not let anyone through the wall, they have built around them. "

"Central points, in order to avoid getting caught in the wrong aims, so is first of all the self-knowledge and then - more importantly - overcome yourself?"

"Yes. But as I said, human has the merciless freedom to make his mistakes. But he also has the chance to live a healthy life and to be satisfied with sufficient resources. "

"So, everything that is unhealthy, as possible to avoid."

"Yes. For example, gluttony, vanity, envy to be a slave to impulses, to resolve the urge to use drugs or conflict with violence.

On the latter: I personally try to resolve conflicts with the head and the feeling - because all history shows: violence generates violence! It follows that violence is not a solution.
In any case, for these growths of life, human often simply gives in to his simple feelings, which serve the respective themes to the point of satisfaction. This is, in two words, light and unhealthy. "

--- frame ---

After another pause, I said, "It can be indescribably beautiful to be left by oneself - more precisely, by one's false aims. If you are in the frame that you have put together yourself and thereby

have a lot of freedom from the negative aims. "

"The frame is basically the constitution
you give yourself - so you can say that
the frame protects you from yourself?"

"Yes. The framework encourages the
positive and mitigates the energy of
the negative aims," I affirmed.

"It is a support you can give yourself
when inappropriate, perhaps extreme,
behaviour could get you into trouble.

Here you can allow, prohibit or restrict
something for a short or long time.

It is important to identify specific
points in time at which you can change
the framework.

And it is also important to get to know
yourself better and better (e.g. what
you (apparently) need)."

"It is built on (self-)knowledge", concluded GP.

"Yes, and in order to be able to react
to changes, it is flexible   in contrast to
the dogmas of religions."

Tolerance

(Conversation about)

With the topics:

> Values
> Introspection
> Acceptance of the world

I was still shaken by what I had just heard.

Of course, one is confronted again and again with intolerant opinions. Here, however, it was this elemental force of emotions that spurred the speaker: "Our faith is the only true, true one. Everyone else is a work of evil and must be fought, eradicated. Only then will we find rest when all believe the truth. "

"How does a person come to believe and spread such a thing?" CP asked me, "because faith is only an opinion, and everyone has their own!"

"There are many reasons," I replied, "a very important one will be the society in which you grew up. Maybe intolerance was taught; that everything that does not live up to its value system is wrong. And must be converted or extinguished.

These people do not even want to find out the values that prevail in other societies in order to understand. They only see their own.

Another reason is often the hot inner feeling that is created by speaking and flooding people, making them become absorbed in their beliefs. When someone is in the strong midpoint of faith, everything else goes by and he can fall into ecstatic rapture. Faith gives these people a feeling of being chosen. And they do not need to use any energy to deal with other beliefs. What else could possibly lead to questioning one's faith more or less. "

"So, these people see the attack on another faith as a defence of their own?"

"Yes - in this case the most primitive: the extinction of the other. But first and foremost, it's about being in the possession of the sole truth and experiencing it."

"'The worst is the belief', I've read somewhere" CP said.

"Well, I would soften it a bit: 'The worst may be faith.' But in fact, when you look at the history of religions, sects, etc., especially in the many periods when violence dominates played, one can turn away with horror. It is faith in particular that can lead to the most inhuman acts, because the interpersonal movements can be eliminated through the midpoint of the faith.

"Many say: 'The most beautiful, faith can be.'"

"Of course, because in faith you can carve exactly the world you want.

Especially religious founders and their subsequent interpreters could wonderfully put together their own world. "

"Did not these people want to make the world better?"

"Above all, they wanted to improve **their** world, chisel their idea of the world in stone, perpetuate it.

Many people do not want change. They want other people to have the same or similar values as they do. They are strangers to everything, try to push it off or fight it.

But faith did not make people "better", but crueller towards others or unbe-lievers. Because as I said, the mid-points can set the compassion to zero.

Because the bad thing is that these believers are absolutely convinced that they are doing the right thing, basking in this feeling. This midpoint of faith can lead to total blindness. He has a tendency to overshadow everything and unfortunately often slides into fa-naticism. And, as everyone can see, he has brought infinite suffering to people throughout history.

The bad thing about faith is the totality with which people can he taken - and want to! When they are totally in the midpoint of the faith, everything goes by around them. And they are looking for that feeling. It envelops them like a bell in which they feel - as in the womb - safe.

--- values ---

Similar intolerance can often be found outside the religion of "normal" people who are convinced of their belief in their own value system and think that everyone else should behave that way."

"Values for man are what he considers important and right?"

"Yeah, especially what his feeling tells him."

"This is probably where conflict is involved," CP interjected, "because everyone has their own value system."

"That's exactly the source of all conflicts between people."

"Compromise and tolerance would be the solution?"

"Yes, but you have to be ready for that."

"You mean to modify your own aims and tolerate the otherness of your counterpart?"

"Exactly. But, as I said, one would first have to be able and willing to understand the values that shape other people.

In any case, the belief that blinds people to the midpoint is often responsible for the greatest catastrophes. The reason is precisely the midpoints that fools man, the world he sees, the values he feels are the only truths. "

"Could you redefine the midpoints?"

"The 'midpoint' is the shape that makes an aim of one."

"And values are aims?"

"Yes.

It does not help, "I continued," to tell these people: 'What you do is one-sided, unreasonable, can be extremely harmful'. These people want to stay in

191

their emotions and often feel as extreme as possible.

So, faith is very resilient. It is an aim that can be deeply rooted in the human being, and that challenges change with tremendous energy. It can - as has been seen countless times in the history of humanity - lead to the worst cruelties to other people. Because, as I said, the midpoints of their faith can nullify compassion. "

"But faith also has positive sides," CP said.

"Of course, I also spoke of the terrible excesses of fanaticism."

"Would not it be better if there was no faith?" CD asked. "Since he has already brought so much misfortune on the people?"

"Certainly, but that is probably impossible, because belief in the broadest sense probably belongs to the equipment in man. Religion seems to be an anchor for people. You can project everything into it, especially your desires.

It is a deep drive in every human being and lie in the primordial structures:

I call it succession-complex: the devotion to someone who is assigned special abilities and who is trusted to the point of blindness.

From this there is, with high probability, the actual cause from which the term "God" was formed.

And that means you can live well - as long as your own faith is not spread by force and other faiths are tolerated. "

--- introspection ---

"But that includes awareness, introspection, and the ability not to indulge in his feelings as soon as they become totalitarian, right?"

"That's the way it is. Unfortunately, faith has strong tendencies to cloud consciousness (better: perception) in the relationship - if only to be sure of self-criticism that could be dangerous to the believer. "

"Do you think that it is ever possible that only one faith, one religion, exists permanently in the world?"

"Never, for that, are the people, and the aims in them too different. In addition, all beliefs split over time into modified beliefs. Because, as I said, people's aims are different.

Religion runs off as an aim as well as all human subjects; through the various sub-aims, the original version that humans generated is differentiated over time."

"So, there will never be peace in matters of faith?"

"Always limited and temporary.

Because there have been, and still are, many people who want to enforce their faith worldwide, who would not find peace until their aim is achieved. Only - these people will never find peace. With this urge that lives in them, they will only produce restlessness, strife, struggle, and cruelty, and even suffer from it. Because violence generates violence. "

He sighed. "But that's the way people are. What happens must happen as it happens."

"In the course of time, some questions arose in me," I said. "Since, as you once said, 'God' is just a structure created in the brain, I ask myself," If faith is so strong in attitude in man, what should one believe in?"

"To yourself and to realization: to detect oneself, the people and the world. Seeing the processes, behaving accordingly and thereby achieving success and satisfaction. "

"Is that your anchor?"

"I believe that what happens has to happen the way it happens. I believe that everyone has their personal value system, that I respect it as best I can. This automatically results in tolerance - and, as a result, relative serenity of the world and of people.

Also, because, as I said, intolerance often leads to incomprehension and subsequently to struggle and violence, because the extreme aims in one want to prevail not infrequently, in the worst case with cruel behaviour. "

--- acceptance of the world ---

He takes a short break. Then he continued.

"Very important is the acceptance of the world. That you can accept what happened as it happened - because it had to happen that way. "

"So here is the tolerance too?"

"Yes, accepting the world - if you cannot change it. This is probably the most important thing for man, because it frees him, does not get bogged down, drives useless struggles. And of course, the acceptance towards yourself.

The reason for the non-acceptance is usually in the rating. "

"So, the value pool that you have in yourself, and from which you see the world, the people and yourself?"

"Yes. The decisive factor is what attitude - above all which basic attitude - you have. One is shaped by it. The attitude is shaped by the inner aims, which in turn form aims that shape one. And especially trigger the emotional reactions. "

"So, you should try to learn to accept the world and the people as they are!"

"Yes - if you can - not to feel yourself, your aims, your values as irrefutable centre of the world. Become able to put them into perspective and thereby be able to adopt other structures."

Self-knowledge

With self-knowledge, one should realize that one is also only a part of the universe, which consists of substances and laws.

It should also make it clear that there is nothing supernatural, metaphysical, mystical, etc. They are merely products of the human brain, which has produced them out of ignorance - and perhaps hubris - in order to explain something to oneself - or to elevate oneself above everything.

In addition, it is important to recognize one's aims - because these are how humans came into being and developed.

An efficient method of self-knowledge is to observe one's feelings; because these have the greatest influence on attitudes and reactions.

Self-control and overcoming

If you get the feeling that you absolutely need something, or that you should do something under all circumstances (which has negative connotations), then you should take a close look at it and ask yourself: where does that come from?

This primarily concerns impulses! The domination - the control - over them by the ego can be particularly important because they can trigger rash, negative actions.

Definition: Impulsivity is a character trait that is characterized by the fact that you follow them. This means that habits have usually already been formed that then run their course.

In this respect, impulses and habits are also an unhappy couple that causes people to always go through the same process.

Impulsivity means that you quickly follow your emotions and thoughts without reflecting on them and assessing the possible consequences. Impulsivity can often also be described as frivolity.

Therefore, you should look at the rising impulse twice (strengthen your perception) before the habit can take hold again.

You should be particularly careful if you feel that a very strong <u>false</u> feeling is developing within you (again) that does not want to allow you to perceive anything else.

You should see this as your last chance to avoid the **'point of no return'**. Because once you are possessed by it, you can no longer turn the pressure around, even if you then perceive it clearly: it holds you captive until the corresponding aim has been satisfied.

You repeatedly experience feelings that tell you 100% that this or that is absolutely right and OK and want to lead you there - sometimes with strong pressure.

The power of feelings can be explained, among other things, by the fact that they have acted as aims related to survival since the emergence of life billions of years ago. They can be found in all areas of living beings.

They work through similarities: If something in the present is similar to a situation in the past, then the feelings urge you to behave today as you did in the past. They are therefore not intelligent and can mislead people.

The psyche consists of midpoints. These carry out the aims in people.

If you want to control yourself, that means: the self forms an aim that uses its center to observe other neural networks and intervenes if they do not function as you want them to. Then, as far as the other aims in the brain allow, it will activate other midpoints that influence the midpoints that have gotten out of control accordingly.

This usually makes sense.

But this can also lead to exaggerations, a certain rigidity that limits the flexibility of the brain.

Because: Excessive self-control carries the risk of self-enslavement. This is often found in "head people" who can only perceive their feelings to a limited extent.

These are people who are more oriented towards the mind of the frontal brain.

On the other hand, too little self-control can be unhealthy because focal points can become overly active.

You can therefore influence yourself by setting aims. Self-observation in particular can help you to influence focal points.

This is stored in the brain and can help you change your own behaviour when similar events occur.

Self-control is a matter of habit or practice.

If you do give in again, however, it would be advisable to think about the process again later. The operator of this aim, the focal point, is currently switched off, so that now, when you look at it soberly, you can also recognize arguments and feelings that were excluded by it.

So, retrospectively getting used to the situation again, reliving these feelings, could make it possible for the future: In similar situations, you act at the same time with the counter-strategy you have developed, which is also primarily driven by feelings that are now being experienced in parallel. And aim to reshape the old.

Once you have separated yourself from unhealthy behaviour, you should keep in mind: These do not disappear forever and ever, but usually only remain in the dark as long as you do not turn to them again - i.e. do them again.

Then it could be more difficult to let go of them again.

Finally, a quick look at good resolutions:

► Why do you make resolutions?

Because something doesn't suit you - and you haven't been able to change it in the long term.

► Why is it so difficult to stick to what you've resolved?

Because all aims have a certain persistence (a life of their own) and want to be fulfilled.

And because habits want to be carried out. They are aims that lure with positive feelings and block out everything that stands in the way of their achievement.

► How do they manage to prevail?

Through the midpoint - mechanism. The pattern of the psyche. This allows them to reduce the value of or block out everything that speaks against them. This includes good resolutions - especially when they are no longer fresh.

▶ How could you change this?

As already mentioned above: By becoming aware of this process, setting an aim that is also activated in the moment.

In other words; When the greed of the wrong target no longer manages to capture all of your attention and you look your inner enemy straight in the eye.

Frame

The framework helps to carry out what one has set out to do, not to deviate from it, thereby increasing self-confidence.

It is a support to give yourself when inappropriate, perhaps extreme, behavior could get you into trouble.

Here you can allow, prohibit or restrict something for a short or long time.

It is important to identify specific points in time at which you can change the framework.

And it is also important to get to know yourself better and better (e.g. what you - apparently - need).

Here's a way if you want to change your own behavior in the future:

1. LOOK AT WHAT YOU DID (THAT WAS ALWAYS! ALSO PERFORMED BY A FEELING AIM IN YOU).

2. LOOK AT WHAT YOU DID NOT WANT.

3. FORM A FEELING COUNTERAIM OF WHAT YOU WANT.

SINCE THE PSYCHE PREFERS TO WORK WITH FEELINGS, ONE SHOULD ALSO DO THIS; BEING AWARE OF YOUR NEGATIVE FEELINGS WHEN VIEWING YOUR UNWANTED BEHAVIOR AND ANCHORING THEM IN RESPECT TO THE POSITIVE FEELINGS, AND RE-MINDER YOURSELF WHEN SUCH A SITUATION OCCURS.

If you broke the frame: write down with what. This reminder helps in similar situations.

When it comes to the past, when it weighs heavily on you, it's always helpful to keep the motto in mind: "What happened had to happen the way it happened."

Also helpful (if you want to get rid of unwanted thoughts and feelings) is the relaxation exercise, as I described it in meditation:

My meditation (relaxation) practice is that as I breathe in, I want to get closer and closer to the end of the universe, and as I breathe out, I want to stay just below that limit I've just reached.

Of course, since the universe is infinite, I can never reach the end. And so I can continue this practice indefinitely.

What is very important: When exhaling, there should be no free space between the "end of the universe" and this limit that I have just reached.

Self-esteem

Self-esteem is the perceived worth that one has of oneself and apparently for other people.

It is generated by one's own aims and by the (apparent) expectations of others.

The midpoint-mechanics plays an essential role here. Because: Everyone wants to feel good about themselves.
If something occurs that could interfere with this, she tries to reinterpret this so that good self-esteem can be maintained.

People are guided by inherited or learned values. These are aims that move you, that you want to achieve in order to be emotionally satisfied.

For example, if you have the aim in yourself - and basically everyone has that - to be recognized by others, and this is not the case, then you will make an effort to achieve this aim in order to have a good self-esteem again.

The resulting positive feeling is an important driving force in people.

Likewise, the ideals that one has of oneself as aims.

Values that trigger corresponding feelings - such as wrong aims - can possibly be transformed through learning by creating a new Target generated.

Condemnation is particularly detrimental to self-esteem; being mad at yourself, curse yourself for doing something wrong, etc.

It can be weakened or avoided by the sentence: What happened had to happen as it happened.

You get a particularly good self-esteem when you have overcome yourself (i.e. aims that act as obstacles to your currently voluntary aim).

And confidence means that you can rely on your psyche without constantly questioning the decisions of your brain.

(You have self-confidence when you trust your psyche).

Contentment and meditation

(Conversation about)

With the topic:

World view (judging)

Revenge

"Could you say when and by what means one is satisfied?" asked GP.

"When you achieve your aims. These are in the brain. It evaluates and signals with feelings whether one has achieved aims, is satisfied or dissatisfied, happy or sad," I replied.

"Moods, such as a bad mood, do not fall from the sky; as a rule, they are dependent on aims that have been achieved or not, which are active within oneself.

So if you know or recognize your aims, you could perceive why you are in the mood you are in."

"Could one say: 'Know your aims, then you know yourself?'"

I nodded. "Exactly, this helps self-knowledge. The advantage is that the brain uses information from consciousness (better: perception) to control itself: for example, creating new aims, deactivating or reactivating old ones, or modifying the aim in question.

As a rule, of course, there is not only one aim, there are various involved, which differ in value. They are more or less different in each person; these are also based on the respective perception and influence the mood".

--- Worldview (judging) ---

"That also goes well with what we were talking about," said GP: "You can look at the world and say: It should be the way I want it to be. Then people evaluate, try to adapt the world to their aims design.

But you can also look at her in such a way that you say: She is what she is; what happens must happen as it happens. Then you don't judge and just accept it.

In the first case, people are constantly trying to shape the world the way they want it to be, trying to change it through various actions, arguments, and fights.
In the second case, he takes her calmly, leaves her as she is."

"Yes," I nodded again. "This also controls satisfaction. It is always linked to the respective aims. People who are constantly trying to shape the world according to their aims and cannot accept it as it is are less likely to be satisfied. Perfectionists have it the hardest. Even idealists don't have it easy."

"But if you want to live by your values, don't you have to change the world?" asked GP.

"The world or yourself. You are right, of course: I, for example, aim for the middle. Between what I want and what I can or must just accept. If I overdo it to one side or the other, then in the long run it's unhealthy, it doesn't reflect life."

"So, it's crucial that you have the right aims in you," reflected GP.

"Or correct them," I added.

"And what are the right aims?"

"Everyone has to decide that for themselves. But it's good to know that you have the opportunity to relax from current midpoints with the sentence: 'What happened had to happen as it happened'. Like anger, for example, whose destructive violence can do a lot of harm.

--- Revenge ---

This also applies in particular to the aim of revenge, which arises, for example, from a violation of the sense of honour and is intended to restore inner contentment. As a rule, however, this becomes a pseudo-satisfaction, because the addressee of the revenge probably also wants to take revenge. You could break this vicious circle by realizing that the past had to happen the way it did, thus saving yourself torment and disharmony.

What happened is often viewed in such a way that one thinks that the other person, the environment, is to blame. Or fate, God, other higher powers would have caused this. Or they would have chosen one for the event themselves. This allows you to completely remove yourself from reality and further fantasies then find plenty of nourishment.

But in the end, it's up to you whether you're satisfied or not: it didn't turn out the way you expected it to – so you had an aim within you – and this triggered your own reactions."

"That means you should first look within yourself to see whether the wrong aims are acting in you and you could change them."

"Yes. Changing your aims also means trying to influence the change in people and the world, i.e. adapting yourself. Because by adapting yourself, you correct or change your aims and your own view of the world."

"Three points can be made, then," concluded GP:

• Satisfaction is achieved by fulfilling one's aims.

• Satisfaction is based on the level of his expectations. It follows that you should not aim for impossible-to-achieve aims. This only creates dissatisfaction and possibly even depression.

• Satisfaction (come to peace) can also be achieved if one says to oneself: What happened had to happen as it happened."

"Meditation can also contribute to satisfaction," GP now remembered. "As far as I know, you do that too."

"Yes," I confirmed, she is focusing on one aim. This weakens others according to the laws of midpoint mechanics.

It is ideal for neutralizing false aims or unfavourable behaviour that has taken root, or for not allowing it to act.

The key is letting go. The essential thing is to perceive the intrusive thoughts and feelings, if they are very strong, but not to respond to them. This gives them neither the space nor the attention they need to develop further.

One could make this clear using the example of falling asleep: thoughts often come to one that one no longer wants to think about. If you go into it, then you are in the center of this respective aim that wants to keep you busy. This is especially the case when fighting against the thoughts. But if you don't do it and return to your aim of falling asleep, then the thoughts lose their value.

This would be a way of defending yourself against intrusive thoughts: do not respond to them and direct your attention or awareness to the center, such as meditation.

Relaxation means that other aims no longer work (other aims than the one you are in at the moment).

The more you practice this, the better it works.

How do you meditate?"

"First of all: All methods in this field aim to focus on something and disregard everything else (such as thoughts and feelings). A crucial point is to perceive something intrusive, especially if it is very strong, but not to engage with it—and of course, not to fight it. This way, you give it neither the space nor the attention it needs to develop further with its midpoints.

I perform my meditation exercise as follows:

Imagine while inhaling:

'Expand your cosmos'

Wait two moments
Then, while exhaling, formulate:

'Deep relaxation'

and add:

'Dissolving in the insubstantial universe'

In fact, there is virtually no room for other thoughts and ideas in this cycle.

Note:

By 'Cosmos' I mean the totality of goals that reside in the psyche of an individual (and control them via neural networks).

The psyche developed over a very long period after life arose from matter and initially had the simple goal of preserving it. It then evolved through increasingly differentiated goals, particularly those required for survival.

Thus, it gradually emerged in the brain through goal-generated neural networks whose function is to control the individual's attitudes toward their inner and outer worlds.

These networks should be as open as possible to allow for adaptation.

Hence the phrase 'Expand your cosmos'; to loosen the boundaries of one's horizon; to keep the limits of one's goals flexible.

In general, this promotes mental agility. Ideally, one is less bound to rigid ideas and unchanging routines, but rather adaptable.

The initial imagining exercise points to this: "Expand your cosmos."

This generally means letting go of rigid goals, attitudes, and structures. Life is in constant flux, and for survival, one should adapt to it. Fixed ideas, as if carved in stone, resist change. This is detrimental to the necessary adaptations to a constantly evolving life.

Anyone striving to install a fixed world in their mind could run into problems sooner or later.

Therefore, one should avoid cementing one's views, opinions, actions, etc. Instead, one should break free from rigid behaviour and judgments and remain as flexible and open as possible to change and expansion.

Again: The psyche, with its goals, is the control center and source of all motivation in a person.

And another comment on "to be absorbed in the (non-representational) universe": Non-representational because the universe cannot be concretely described, but only from a perspective.

Meditation is excellent for focusing attention. And incidentally, without any further effort, all other core focus

is enhanced through this technique."
reduced.

And, as mentioned: Without exception, all relaxation techniques utilize the withdrawal of attention by focusing on something else (as in the form described here)."

I thought about it. Then I continued: There is a theory about meditation that seems very plausible to me:
"The state of meditation is created by brain processes. It begins with the aim of eliminating all thoughts, feelings, and perceptions. So it is very important to stop the incessant chattering of thoughts. Concentrating on this creates lively neuron activity in the attention center of the brain. This signals to slow down the flow of neural information. As a result, an area that is responsible for our orientation in space is increasingly cut off from neuronal impulses. If the area lacks the necessary stimuli, it only remains to create the subjective impression of complete spacelessness, which is interpreted as infinite space and eternity. Another area is responsible for imagining the limitations of our body. The total blackout of signals on this side means the perception of oneself

becomes limitless. As the meditation deepens, the boundary between the inner and outer world blurs, and there is a sense of expansion and merging with the environment. By concentrating on one point, the flood of information from which people derive their orientation disappears. As a result, the boundary between the ego and the world also disappears, the feeling of oneness with the world and of limitlessness sets in. In the deepest meditation one has the feeling of becoming one with the universe, of becoming one with something very much greater to dissolve."

For a very deep meditation, you usually have to practice long and hard."

"And all this only happens in the brain?"

"Of course, but the meditator actually has the feeling of being one with everything. This state is sought. It is not uncommon to find people who vehemently resist such a materialistic interpretation among those who have already had this experience of 'boundless oneness with everything'. They just can't and don't want to imagine that it's just happening in their brain because it was such an overwhelming experience. Perhaps they fear that they will not be able to experience this again with a similar intensity if they would admit that everything consists only of substances and laws and that there is no metaphysical power behind it.

 "Do you have to believe in mysticism to meditate deeply?"

"No. But of course you can also immerse yourself in mystical fantasies. However, I personally prefer to keep both feet on the ground during meditation.

Epilogue

> **Finally, I would like to remind you in particular of these 3 natural foundations by which we are (willed or not) shaped:**

1. Deep drives in every human being

▶ *Life complex:* To live as long as you can, regardless of the circumstances.

▶ *Producer complex:* The mainspring to produce offspring, regardless of the environmental conditions.

▶ *Succession complex:* The devotion to someone who is assigned special abilities and who is trusted to the point of blindness.

<u>**2. God**</u>

From the last (succession complex), there is, with high probability, the actual cause from which the term "God" was formed.

As a rule, it is difficult to escape the feelings that have formed and embedded in the psyche from the beginning of the multicellular life to the present.

It would be helpful to use human cognitive abilities; But even with this, these feelings are often difficult to influence.

3. Naturally predetermined

That everything had to come as it came is proven from two sides:

▶Identic parts under identical circumstances **always** result in identical structures.

▶The statistical calculation of probability enables mathematicians to make very precise predictions about quantum systems. This would not be feasible if lawlessness prevailed here.

And something else essential:

It is often forgotten that people are only living beings that developed from inorganic substances and, like these, are shaped by laws. The main difference between inorganic and organic substances is **the aim of survival.**

The main difference between humans and other living beings is their brain, which is capable of forming exorbitant networks of neurons, with which they can recognize laws and create new processes.

And - with which an infinite number of imaginative structures can be fooled into him.

Such as the alleged role of consciousness:

In fact, up until the 23rd century, it was believed that consciousness is the real (objective) perception of the world believed to be from the human point of view, which the brain then absorbs:

Namely, that the environment sends stimuli that people's senses pick up and direct them to the inside of the brain, which uses them to recognize the world.

With this picture he would then have made his free decisions.

This kind of perception has never been scientifically proven.

In the end:

> Let me add a few basic words about the relationship between my (potential) readers and myself:
>
> People are guided by aims. These can or are influenced by the mid-point-mechanics. In such a way that what speaks against them is less or not at all noticed.
>
> As a rule, you do not notice these processes because they are part of the routine that the brain carries out on a daily basis.

This influence applies to a relatively large part of my representations regarding the perception of the readers.

For most, this is a description that doesn't fit their image of humanity.

That is unfortunate.

But I'm not interested in serving such expectations, but in writing what I've learned through my research.

Constructive criticism
is welcome.

Other books by me:

- Blindheit der Klugen
- Blindness of the wise
- Mittelpunkt der Psyche
- Midpoint of the psyche
- Die Entzauberung des Bewusstseins (geänderte Auflage)
- The disenchantment of consciousness
- Was Gläubige wissen sollten
- What Believers Should Know
- Die Nicht-Entstehung des Universums
- The non-creation of the universe
- Wutgefühle: (Wie Gefühle entstanden und den Menschen bewegen)
- Die Welt ohne Metaphysik: (Eine klare Sicht auf den Menschen und die Welt)
- The world without metaphysics: (A clear view of human and the world)
- 3 Gründe: Psychologische Grundlagen des Menschen ●●● Physikalische Grundlagen der Welt ●●● Betrachtungen des Glaubens
- 3 Basics of human beings